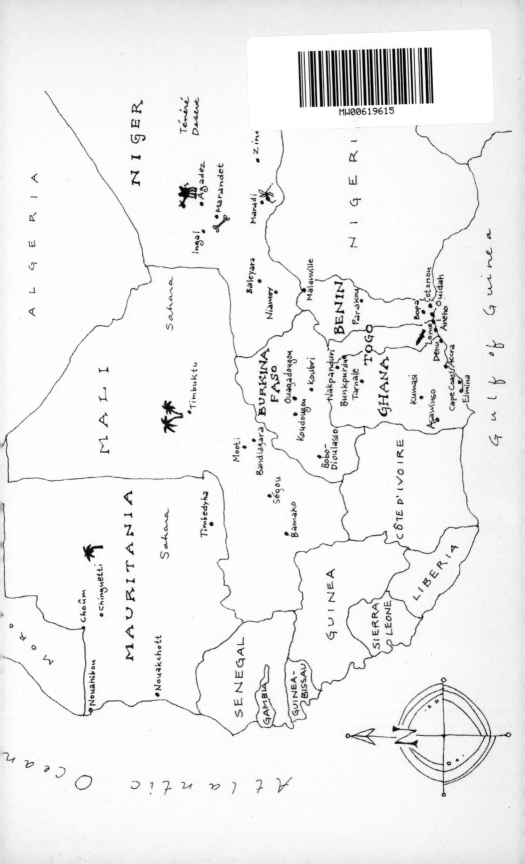

Harmattan

Wind Across West Africa

Marcelo D. Cut

Harmattan

Wind Across West Africa

a travelogue by

Marcello Di Cintio

INSOMNIAC PRESS

Edited and designed by Jan Barbieri
Copy edited by Adrienne Weiss
Map drawn by Jen Chic

National Library of Canada Cataloguing in Publication

Di Cintio, Marcello, 1973–
Harmattan : wind across West Africa / Marcello Di Cintio.

ISBN 1-894663-32-2

1. Di Cintio, Marcello, 1973- --Journeys--Africa, West. 2. Africa, West--Description and travel. I. Title.

DT472.D52 2002 916.604'329 C2002-903811-1

The publisher gratefully acknowledges the support of the Canada Council, the Ontario Arts Council and the Department of Canadian Heritage through the Book Publishing Industry Development Program.

Printed and bound in Canada

Insomniac Press,
192 Spadina Avenue, Suite 403,
Toronto, Ontario, Canada, M5T 2C2
www.insomniacpress.com

THE CANADA COUNCIL | LE CONSEIL DES ARTS
FOR THE ARTS | DU CANADA
SINCE 1957 | DEPUIS 1957

ONTARIO ARTS COUNCIL
CONSEIL DES ARTS DE L'ONTARIO

for Gabrielle

Ghana: Denu

When people ask me why I'm going to West Africa I always lie. I tell them I am attracted to a place where few travellers go, places most people can't find on a map. I talk about my friends' travels in Asia and India, how they inspired me, and how I want different stories to tell. Sometimes I tell them I am following in the steps of my grandfather who went to Africa with the Italian army in World War II—though he fought in Egypt, far away from my journey. Other times I talk about African culture, the music and religion, the refreshing simplicity of existence. Or I invent a lifelong yearning for the Sahara Desert that had to be satisfied. I like sounding adventurous, romantic, sentimental, poetic.

These are reasons for staying for ten months, and reasons to return, but they are not leading me to West Africa.

Two summers ago I took a date to an Ethiopian restaurant after reading a review in a Calgary newspaper. The restaurant, called The Teff, was located in a strip mall between a paint supply store and a Seven-Eleven. It went out of business less than a year after opening. Heather and I had a wonderful meal at The Teff. We were the only diners in the restaurant that afternoon. Our server, a beautiful Ethiopian woman, patiently described

*what we were eating and how to scoop the stew with our hands in a piece
of injera bread. At the end of the meal we shared a small pot of spiced coffee
and argued who would take the leftovers home. Afterwards I decided to
visit Africa.*

*I don't want to admit a meal in a strip mall restaurant led me to Africa.
I don't want to gild an eighteen dollar lunch with such significance. There
is no romance in that.*

As the plane touched down in Ghana's Kotoka Airport in the capital city of Accra, I felt an immense sense of relief. It was the end
of April and eight months of fundraising and orientation prefaced
this moment. Africa, finally, was just outside the airplane door.

I stepped out of my seat, pulled my small daypack from the
overhead bin and stood in the aisle, waiting for the cabin to depres-
surize. The other volunteers chattered nervously, but I was too
excited to say anything. Two of the volunteers were so worked up
they started to cry. Some of the Ghanaian passengers laughed at
them and I was moderately embarrassed. I couldn't see past the
head of the person in front of me, but I heard the hatch open and
felt a breeze from outside rush into the plane. The air was hot and
damp and thick. I started to sweat—partly from the heat and partly from anticipation.

We inched forward through the cabin unbearably slow. When I
finally reached the threshold I expected to see Ghana, but instead
I saw black tarmac, the terminal's flashing lights, luggage being
heaved onto carts by airport workers and night sky all around. I
wanted to step outside of the plane into the Africa of my imagination. I wanted to squint into the sun and see swaying palms, women
carrying pails of water on their heads. I wanted to see elephants
and the pages of *National Geographic*. But it was nearly midnight
and in the darkness this could have been any airport in the world.
Africa was out there but I couldn't tell. It was illogical, I know, but
I felt disappointed, cheated by the night.

The first thing we did when we stepped off the airplane was to cheer and hug each other, as if simply arriving was an accomplishment. The next thing we did, because we were all Canadians, was comment on the weather.

"It sure is hot," said one of the volunteers.

"And it's the middle of the night."

"Can you imagine the heat in the day?"

Jennifer pulled a camera from her carry-on and lifted it to her eye.

"Everybody smile."

I reached out and pushed the camera away before anyone assembled. Jennifer looked hurt and confused.

"What did you do that for?"

"It's against the law to take pictures in airports here," I said.

"Why?"

"I don't know. Something to do with the airport being a strategic building. Photos can be used to plan a coup or something."

"How do you know that?"

"I think I read it in my guidebook." I felt like the smartest person there.

We entered the terminal, and while the rest of our group retrieved their baggage, I ducked into a restroom. I had waited for this moment for hours, avoiding the airplane toilets because they scare me a little bit. I reasoned the airport must have comfy bathroom facilities. I was wrong.

There were three stalls inside the restroom and I chose the only one with a door. In my haste I didn't notice the lack of toilet paper until I was nearly finished. I searched for scraps of tissue in my pockets but found nothing, and a mild panic began to set in. I suddenly didn't feel so smart.

After a moment or two of deliberation I removed my boots and slid off my pants and boxer shorts. I tore the boxers into two pieces; this was difficult as they were brand new. I had new boxers, new hiking boots, new trim haircut. I had to use my teeth to rip the seams. I laughed to myself as the button on the fly came loose, clicked on the linoleum and rolled under the neighbouring stall. I wiped myself with my torn underwear, put on my pants and boots, exited the stall and tossed the ball of soiled rags into an overflowing trash bin. I rinsed my hands in the sink and dried them on my pants before returning to the others, feeling victorious.

The first Africans I met were a gang of thieves. Richard, the Ghanaian volunteer coordinator, was supposed to meet all the volunteers outside and ferry us to our hotel, but none of us knew what he looked like. When we stepped outside the terminal we were mobbed by about twenty young men. They surrounded us and tried to pull the bags from our backs. Some claimed to be baggage handlers and tried to talk us into giving them our luggage. Others didn't bother lying and simply jammed their hands into our pockets to probe for wallets. Somewhere in the throng of bodies was Richard, but over the shoving and arguing, we couldn't tell which one he was.

The shouting increased until a huge Ghanaian man with massive fists grabbed one of the thieves, shouted at him in a language I didn't understand, and shoved him to the ground. He took another boy by the neck and with two extended fingers poked him in the eyes, Three Stooges-style. The boy screamed and jumped back. The man shouted to us: "I am Richard. I have come to meet you." I was relieved he was on our side.

Richard and his friends continued to battle the "baggage handlers." In the melee, one of the volunteers, Anita, was pushed to the ground. She started to cry. I bent to help her up and immediately felt a hand in my pocket; these were clumsy thieves. I reached down and grabbed the thief by the wrist, pulled his hand from my pocket and spun around to face him. He was a boy of about fifteen, wearing a filthy T-shirt and torn blue jeans. I tightened a fist and, inspired by Richard, got ready to punch it into his face. But the boy just stood there. He didn't try to pull his hand free or run away. He stared into my eyes with a look that said, "You caught me. So what?" I froze. The boy's face was so devoid of aggression that my violence seemed inappropriate. I let go of his wrist because I couldn't think of anything better to do. He gave me a quick grin and casually walked away, as if we had just shaken hands.

A man touched me on the shoulder and said, "Please. Put your bags in the back of the car." He pointed to a line of three Peugeot station wagons. One had its back hatch opened. I didn't know if we could trust this man so I looked to Richard. He was holding one of the thieves by his shirt collar. He paused and shouted to me, "Yes. Yes. He is with us. You put your bags in the car and we go." Then he tore the boy's shirt off and punched him in the nose. I tossed my bag into the back and stood guard while the other volunteers did the same. The thieves, weary from fighting, started to back off. We piled into the three cars and made our getaway.

We spent a week sequestered in a guest house in Tema, a town that is a few kilometres outside Accra, for an orientation. Richard was charged with teaching us a few things about Ghana before we embarked on our individual volunteer placements. I was one of ten volunteers with Canadian Crossroads International, a volunteer outfit that sends Canadians abroad to "foster global understanding."

I had been overseas before—I travelled to Italy on a family vacation and visited France for a couple weeks in my senior year of high school—but that doesn't count. Europe doesn't count, especially not while under the watchful eyes of parents and Catholic school chaperones. This was my first real travelling experience. I wanted to be challenged. I wanted to get dirty for the first time. Crossroads supplied my ticket, and the three months I spent volunteering and living with a Ghanaian family was to be my training and my cultural decompression chamber. Then I planned to strap on my too-clean backpack and see Africa with my own eyes. I had already cancelled my return ticket before I left Canada. I planned to be gone ten months.

Before I left Calgary a friend asked me if I was going to Africa to find myself. "Why would I find myself in Africa," I said. "I'm a white man from Canada. I'm going to lose myself." My grandmother said I wouldn't last three months.

Crossroads selects volunteers for their openness to "cross-cultural experiences," but at the guest house, when we all sat down for our first Ghanaian lunch, all we experienced was panic.

The restaurant menu, printed in fading ink and enclosed in plastic report covers, was filled with unrecognizable, and mostly unpronounceable, dishes. Our orientation weekends back in Canada never prepared us for this. Were "garden eggs" the same as chicken eggs? What were groundnuts? How do you say *nkatenkwan*? Feigning bravery I asked the waitress for a plate of fish and *palava*, whatever that was. The others did the same, ordering by pointing at items on the menu they could not pronounce. Only Anita betrayed her fear by ordering the single Western item on the menu, spaghetti bolognese. "I just want to see how they make it in Africa," she said when we scolded her cowardice.

We waited an age for our food and ignored the glasses of water our waitress provided, certain they were contaminated with deadly tropical diseases. When she brought our food, the aroma defeated our already shaky sense of adventure.

"This smells really weird."

"What do you suppose this is?" Jennifer said, staring at a plate filled with rice and something.

"This is chicken, but what are these bits in the sauce?"

Jodi earned groans from the rest of the group when she said her dish smelled like cat food. We poked at our meals with tentative forks, and it was a long time before anybody tried anything. When we did, we ate very, very slowly. My *palava*, a mix of greens and crushed melon seeds, was tasty, but the fish wasn't scaled or gutted and I quickly gave up on it.

"This is great but I'm so full," I lied and pushed away my half-eaten meal. Nobody finished except for Anita who slurped up every last strand of her pasta.

That night, after a dinner where half the volunteers ordered spaghetti bolognese, Richard took us to an outdoor bar to drink giant bottles of Ghanaian beer and snack on peanuts. Richard called them groundnuts and this solved one of the day's menu mysteries. While we took turns calling our mothers from a nearby phone booth, Richard answered our questions about Ghana and tried to teach us a few phrases of the local language. The next morning, however, the only word I remembered was *bubra*, the local word for draught beer.

I got up and headed for the bathroom. When I opened the door, I saw a three-inch-long lizard in the window well of the shower. I called out to Ben, my roommate, who rushed in to investigate.

"Wow! That's so great! Let me go tell the others."

Before long the bathroom was crowded with volunteers wanting a glimpse of the local fauna. Anne and Jennifer brought their cameras.

"That is so disgusting!"

"I think it's cute."

"Why isn't it moving? Is it dead?"

"Marcello, poke it and see if it moves."

"No thanks."

"You're not going to shower with that thing in there, are you?"

"Why? Do lizards bite?"

"I don't think so."

"I wish there was a lizard in my shower."

"Marcello, stand beside it and I'll take a picture," Jennifer said pulling the lens cap off her camera.

I posed next to the lizard, who seemed oblivious to all the excitement he had caused, and waited for the flash. The lizard never moved but the crowd of volunteers finally dispersed. I showered quickly, keeping my eye on the lizard at all times.

After breakfast Richard chartered a minivan, or *tro-tro*, to bring us into Accra. We lined up at the immigration office to extend our visas, and then registered at the Canadian Embassy. A well-tanned official warned us against smoking marijuana and spoke quickly about Ghanaian voodoo, or *juju*, beliefs.

"*Juju* is real only if you believe in it," he said. "If you don't believe, then you are safe."

This comment didn't make much sense to me, and I didn't know how to follow his advice. How can reality depend on belief instead of the other way around?

We left the embassy and Richard took us to the Novotel, a chic downtown hotel where we converted our traveller's cheques into Ghanaian *cedis*. One hundred Canadian dollars yielded a thick wad of currency that was difficult to stuff into our money belts. The lumps of cash protruding from our waists nullified the deception of our "hidden" travel wallets.

As the ultimate test of our newly acquired survival skills, Richard abandoned us in Accra and let us find our own way back to the guest house. I'm sure he intended for us to find a public *tro-tro* headed in the right direction, crowd on with a group of locals and have the presence of mind to know where to get off. Most of us, though, simply chartered the first taxi we flagged down, paid an extortionate fare and got dropped at the front door. Richard was disappointed and called us "soft."

After five days of orientation, I felt myself getting restless. The seclusion of the guest house was claustrophobic. We had little chance to meet any Ghanaians, except the guest-house staff and the occasional visitor who dropped by for a drink on the garden patio. (One of these guests, named William Brown, Sr., claimed to have brought rock and roll to Ghana.) I was uneasy about starting my placement but weary of travelling in a herd of Westerners— large groups make me feel clumsy.

The week would have been unbearable if it wasn't for Anne, a volunteer from Victoria. We chased lizards in the garden, and when it rained for the first time, we rushed into the courtyard, turned our faces upwards and danced in the downpour. The guest-house staff shook their heads and laughed at our laughing.

When we were together, like on the last night of orientation week, I felt at home and not so clumsy. Anne and I escaped from our rooms after dark, climbed to the roof of the guest house and stared into the sky until morning. We talked about our lives in Canada, about Anita, who was afraid to leave her bedroom that morning, and the lizards in the garden. But mostly we talked about how, after so many months of anticipation, we couldn't believe we were in Ghana. We said it over and over again: "I can't believe we are here. I can't believe this is Africa." We were both so shocked and thrilled. She laid her head on my chest and let me hold her hand, but the setting hardly inspired romance. The corrugated roof was dirty and the moon and stars could not pierce the rain clouds. The night air was scented by diesel fumes from the highway and the acrid stench of the mosquito repellent we had applied in paranoid doses. As we stared into the horizon to watch the sunrise, we realized too late that we were facing west instead of east.

The next morning all the volunteers said goodbye to each other, exchanged addresses and found transport to the villages that would be our homes for the next three months. Richard flagged down a public *tro-tro* headed to Denu, a seaside town near the Togo border, and helped me aboard. He gave instructions to the driver then turned to me: "Safe journey."

The driver knew the road well and piloted his *tro-tro* on the torn highway as if by instinct. On smooth stretches he accelerated until the engine screamed, then braked suddenly on the edge of potholes. These wounds in the asphalt, revealing red soil underneath like open sores, were the only obstacles that slowed the driver down. Even when we passed through villages he leaned on his horn to clear the path of people and animals, while his sandalled foot never left the gas pedal. The ride was exciting and dangerous, and I sat forward in my seat to anticipate each bump. The Ghanaian passengers were hardly aroused and some, impossibly, slept even as the vehicle bounced down the highway. Rain fell so hard I imagined the drops were adding fresh cracks to the windshield.

I sat in the middle of the *tro-tro*, surrounded by Africans. We travelled at blurring speeds, yet each time we passed a group of children on the side of the road they noticed me and waved. What sharp eyes they had for white-fleshed strangers.

When I arrived at the Denu junction I took a taxi to Three Town Senior Secondary School. I knew little about my volunteer placement, only that I would teach a semester there and my host father was the headmaster. I didn't even know what subject I would teach.

There were three women selling groundnuts and little baggies of drinking water near the entrance to the schoolyard.

"Excuse me," I said. "I am a teacher here and I am looking for

Mr. Quansah."

One of the women shouted something to a teenaged boy who was reading against a tree nearby. He put down his book and led me into a small house on the school campus.

"You sit and I will go and get my father."

"You are Mr. Quansah's son?"

"Yes."

"You are my brother, then. My name is Marcello. I will be staying here for a few months."

"Yes, I know. We are waiting for you. I am Kwashie. You are welcome." He walked out of the house.

I sat down and tried to memorize some phrases in the local language from my guidebook, hoping to impress my host father when he arrived. The door opened and Kwashie entered carrying two half-litre bottles of beer: Guiness Export. He opened both bottles and placed them on the table in front of me. Then he fetched a single glass from the kitchen.

"Are these both for me?" I asked pointing at the beers. It was ten in the morning.

Kwashie nodded.

"That's a lot of beer."

"Yes," he smiled.

"Thank you."

"Don't mention."

I glanced down at my language guide and said, "*Ah ta sen?*" Kwashie looked confused. I repeated, "*Ah ta sen?*"

He shook his head. "Sorry. I do not understand."

"It means 'How are you?' doesn't it? '*Ah ta sen?*'" I showed him my book and he followed across the page with his finger.

"Ah. These are Twi words. We do not speak Twi here. We speak Ewe."

"Oh."

"I will go get my father," he said and left the house. I looked back at my guidebook. There was no language guide for Ewe.

The beer was thick and foul—it seemed as if Guiness didn't export its finest brew to West Africa. Still, by the time the headmaster arrived I'd finished one of the beers, had started the second and was mildly buzzed. The headmaster was a small man in his forties. His hair was short and neatly trimmed, and he had a scar below his left eye. He wore a shirt and trousers made of the same pinstriped grey cloth, with black socks and black shoes.

"You are Marcello? I am Mr. Quansah, the headmaster." He reached out to shake my hand, and when he released the handshake, he snapped his fingers against mine. "This is how we shake hands in Ghana," he said. "I will teach you. *Wazo*."

"*Wazo*," I said back.

He grinned. "No. *Wazo* means 'welcome.' When someone says *wazo* you say 'yo.'"

"*Yo*," I said.

"Good. Now you know Ewe." He sat down on the sofa across from me. "Do you like the beer? I know Canadians like beer. Last year we had another volunteer come here. Trevor. Do you know him?"

"No. But I've heard of him."

"Trevor was a very funny man. He looked like you a little bit. But he was taller. Very funny. Every day he would drink two bottles of Guiness. He said it is good for you." He laughed again, a chuckle that spilled out the sides of his mouth.

"Do you want some of my beer?" I asked. "One bottle is enough for me."

"No. I don't like Guiness. You finish. It is good for you." He paused to laugh, then said, "Last year Trevor taught English here at Three Town. I was going to let you do the same, but I looked at your information and it said you have a degree in biology. I think you should teach biology instead. Okay?"

"That's fine with me."

"Okay. I will send for the head of the science department to meet with you and give you materials. You will be teaching the form one students. Are you a teacher in Canada?"

"No. This will be my first teaching job. I'm a bit nervous."

"You will be fine. Do not worry. "

"Are there any other foreign teachers at Three Town?"

"No, you are the only one. I also read that you were a wrestler in Canada. Is this true?"

"Yes. I was on the wrestling team in high school and at my university."

"But you are so small."

"Some wrestlers are smaller than me," I said, feeling indignant and noticing I probably outweighed Mr. Quansah by ten pounds.

"Is that so?" He paused to think on it for a moment then stood up. "Okay. What do you want to do right now? We can go for a tour and you can meet some of your students."

I followed Mr. Quansah around the schoolyard. Three Town's campus consisted of five small buildings and a soccer field flanked by two wobbly goalposts. Most of the buildings were made of stone with corrugated steel roofs and large open windows. Unlike the roads in the village, the school grounds were free of trash and impeccably tidy. Even the sandy patches in the soccer field seemed to be brushed flat and even. The students, too, were dressed in smart turquoise uniforms. The boys wore short-sleeved shirts with matching shorts, and the girls wore fitted sleeveless dresses. Each time the headmaster and I passed a classroom the students nudged each other, whispered and pointed our way. My arrival was the source of some excitement, or at least distraction, and I suddenly felt self-conscious.

Mr. Quansah brought me into a classroom where a teacher was giving a lecture about basic chemistry. When we walked into the door the entire class of about forty students started chatting happily. The teacher stepped aside as the headmaster introduced me to the class.

"This is Mr. Marcello. He will be teaching form one biology for the rest of the term. He is from Canada."

"Welcome," they said in unison.

"Yo," I said. Everyone giggled.

The headmaster turned to me. "Now you can introduce yourself, if you like."

Nervous, I walked to the front of the class and told everyone my name again. I wrote it on the board because I thought that's what teachers do. I told them I was from Canada and that I studied biology at a university in Calgary. I didn't tell them I'd never taught before, or that I was a wrestler in Canada. When my short introduction was complete, I looked back to the headmaster.

"Is that all?" he asked.

"I think so."

"Do you want to teach?"

"You mean right now?"

"Why not?"

"Isn't there a class going on already?"

The chemistry teacher shrugged. "It is okay. Go ahead."

"But I don't know what to teach. I'm not really prepared."

"It is no problem. Teach anything you like." He handed me a piece of chalk.

I turned to face the students. Each was smiling and anticipating a spontaneous lesson. "Does anyone have any questions?" I asked. "About biology?"

Every hand went up.

"I am taking you on a tour of Denu," Fred said. He was a mathematics teacher at the school and was excited to show me around. We walked around the village and stopped to greet nearly every person we passed. Fred showed me the post office, the marketplace and the district office for teachers.

"You can go there," he said, "because you are a teacher, too." He held my hand as we walked. This is common practice among males in Ghana, even between casual acquaintances. I remembered this custom was mentioned in my orientation, but it felt strange to me. I took every opportunity to casually release his grip. I had thought I was more open-minded.

We passed three elderly men sitting next to a rough concrete building. Unlike the rest of the men I saw, these three were wearing turbans. I waved at them and they smiled and nodded their heads, but Fred didn't introduce me.

"Who are those men?" I asked.

Fred scowled. "Those are Muslims. They smell bad because they never wash."

"Are there many Muslims in Denu?"

"No. Only those three old men. All day long they sit next to their mosque and do nothing." He turned to me. "What is your religion?"

"My parents are Catholic, but I really don't follow any particular faith anymore."

"Why not?"

"I don't know." I stumbled on my words. "I guess I don't really believe anymore."

"I will take you to church on Sunday," he said.

On a side street we passed a strange white sculpture. It looked like a lump of rounded stone, sheltered under a small lean-to made of dried palm fronds. In front of the sculpture were two broken wooden bowls; one contained a white liquid, the other a few cooked beans. When I asked Fred about the sculpture, he seemed to get nervous, as if I was asking him to reveal a secret.

"That is the fetish shrine for Denu."

"What do you mean?"

"It is our beliefs, like *juju*. Some people, when they need something, they make a sacrifice to the fetish, and the spirit will give them what they wish."

"What kind of sacrifices do they make?"

"You see in the bowls? There is some food and some palm wine."

"Who makes these sacrifices?"

"Everybody does."

"Really? Even the Muslims?"

"Yes. Sometimes."

"What about you? Have you ever done this?"

He paused before answering. "Yes. Sometimes. If I need something."

"And you are a Christian, right?"

"Yes. Of course."

I asked if I could take a picture of the shrine, but Fred said it would not be appropriate.

We ended up at Fred's home and reclined on grass mats behind his house. His sandy yard was outlined by a leaning fence of woven palm leaves and a coconut palm grew in the middle. He knocked down three coconuts with a long pole, hacked at them with a machete and urged me to drink the milk.

"If you drink plenty of coconut water you will never get malaria," he said. Afterwards he asked if I wanted some *akpeteshie*.

I had tried *akpeteshie* at the guest house in Tema. After dinner one night Richard presented a bottle of clear liquid.

"This is *akpeteshie*," he'd said. "It is Ghanaian whisky made from palm wine. It is very hot, very strong. Everybody in Ghana will want you to drink it, so we will try some tonight so you know what it is like."

Richard had filled a two-ounce glass and passed it around the table so everybody could take a sip. It was strong, but pleasant tasting. Judging from Richard's description I had expected something far more foul. I'd tried bargain tequila in Calgary that makes *akpeteshie* taste like skim milk.

"I'd love some," I said to Fred.

Fred seemed pleased and pulled a bottle from a cabinet. He filled a six-ounce glass and handed it to me.

My eyes bulged. "This is all for me?"

"Of course."

"Fred, I can't drink all of this."

"Why not? You like *akpeteshie*?"

"Yes I like it, but—" I started to laugh. "I don't think I can drink this much."

"Ah, it is too strong for you. Should I dilute it?"

I nodded and Fred took away my glass and poured the *akpeteshie* into a larger cup. Then he reached for another bottle from the cabinet and topped up the drink with a reddish liquid.

"What are you diluting it with?" I asked.

"Red wine."

I laughed again and took the glass. The wine did little to dilute the *akpeteshie*, and now it tasted disgusting, but I felt foolish complaining again. I smiled and thanked him.

I finished about half the glass before a thick red haze washed over me. I'd never buzzed like this before and felt more high than drunk. Denu started to spin around me so fast I feared the coconut palm would uproot. Thankfully Fred suggested we take a midday nap. I waited until he fell asleep before tossing the remaining cocktail onto the ground. I swept sand over the spill then passed out with my legs on a grass mat and my face in the dirt.

In the days that followed, my feelings of awkwardness and novelty began to fade. The Ghanaian sun melted them away as quickly as it burned my skin. Before long, my life in Denu developed a daily routine.

Most days I woke to crowing roosters, barking dogs, morning porridge and CNN's Hollywood update: summer movies I would never see. Then I would teach two short biology classes to teenagers who barely understood my accent much less the mechanics of photosynthesis. I was something of a novelty to them, the new white teacher who spoke gibberish about cytoplasm and osmosis and pronounced his Rs funny. They looked up at me attentively yet blankly, respecting my authority but not understanding a word.

After my classes I would sit with the three home science teachers, who quickly became my adoptive mothers. They fussed about my Caucasian hair and North American clothes, ridiculed my Ewe, and marvelled at my contact lenses: "Can I try them in my eyes?" They would sit with me for hours, often neglecting their own classes, to chat about Canada, my family, and why I was twenty-four and still not married: "You will marry my daughter and take her to Canada. She is a very good cook, and very pretty." Over glasses of corn ale—a sweet, non-alcoholic drink that drove the flies mad— they would ask me questions that made me laugh: "Are you short because the area you live in is very hilly?" And others that made me nervous: "Is AIDS real? Our husbands tell us it is not." I'd ask them about *juju* and they would get nervous too.

In the afternoon I would wander down the main dirt road that ran through Denu. I'd pass the "drinking bar" next to the school where I would often stop for an afternoon beer or Africola, then pass the auto-parts shop and the three quiet Muslims in front of their crude cement mosque. One of the town crazies might jog by wearing only tattered underwear. Along the road women would be selling small, cellophane-wrapped balls of groundnuts or tiger nuts, bottles of red palm oil or *akpeteshie*. A cart full of coconuts might be pushed along by a trio of boys, who'd stop and pose for my camera. I would see a sign hung from the wall of a private house: "Cat soup served here." A taxi might rattle by with seven passengers and no windows. Through the exhaust I'd see two bumper stickers: one depicting pop singer Madonna from her black lace "Lucky Star" days, the other spelling out "I am covered in the Blood of Christ" in red, dripping letters.

A man might call out to me, "White boy! Where is my money?" Another might yell, "Mr. Canada! Give me your T-shirt!" Two naked babies would play in a puddle, eating mud. I'd see a chicken hung upside down from a bicycle on his way from the market. (Did he realize his day wasn't going to get any better?) Another child would scream at my alien whiteness and bury his head in his mother's knees. She would laugh and tell him that if he misbehaved, the white monster would take him away. A shirtless crazy woman might pass, howling curses at the invisible tormentors that followed her around town.

I would greet the village chief, who owned the drugstore next to the post office. He also ran a telephone booth and, according to Claire the sewing teacher, raised cats for soup.

Usually, two women would be pounding *fufu* nearby. They would labour over a giant wooden mortar filled with mashed boiled cassave. One woman would stand upright and work the *fufu* stick, a two-metre pestle with a rounded end. She'd hold the stick with both hands and pound it into the mortar with deft, downward strokes. The other woman would kneel beside the mortar and turn over the ball of pulverized dough between each hit, her hands working quickly to escape the mortar just before the *fufu* stick came crashing down. In Ghana, even cooking sounded like drumming.

I'd buy a snack—usually a "meat" kebab from the grill boy at the junction, or a small bag of tiger nuts at the stand in front of the police post—and hope that my host mother wouldn't spot me. She would be embarrassed if she thought I was underfed. I'd retreat with my contraband to the seashore where I'd sit against coconut palms or beached fishing boats with sayings like *Mawu li* (God is here) brightly painted on their hulls. I'd spend hours eavesdropping on waves, or devouring Victorian-era British novels from the school library. I might read *Pride and Prejudice* while young girls came to the beach to shit. On the way home I'd pick up a pineapple for dessert from the woman who sat next to Word of Jehovah Beauty Salon.

At night, after dinner, pineapple and the local news, I'd scribble letters to Anne or friends abroad who also wondered how such a place could exist. Often I'd walk to Hotel Vilcabamba on the edge of town for a beer. There was an old, out of tune piano there that the staff let me play. Other times I'd sit with the owner, Tom, and we'd talk about sex. He thought of little else. Tom had been to London and developed a taste for white women. "White meat," he called them. Then I would go home to bed before the gate was locked and the dogs were let out.

As the days passed I became a familiar face to the villagers. I started to learn their names: Dofi, the hairdresser; Mr. Frimpong at the post office and his son Kpedo. They started to call me by name, too, but since "Marcello" was difficult for them to pronounce, I was baptized with a whole array of new names.

After three weeks I heard "Marcello" corrupted to "Machallo," "Marshallow" or, oddly enough, "Marshay-Marshay." Ghanaians receive a name according to the day of the week they were born, and my Saturday birthday earned me the moniker "Kwame." This was often changed to "Kwame-vi," which means "little Kwame"; it was important, I guess, to distinguish me from normal-sized Kwames. Children called me *"yavu,"* Ewe slang for white man, although the direct translation was "tricky dog." Sometimes they sang "*yavu, yavu, gai-bo*" (white man, white man, black chin), in reference to my goatee. Other people called me "White Man" in English. I was also "Short Man" and worse, "Small Boy," but I never responded to these.

My favourite name, though, was "Canada Man." It sounded like a superhero.

Many of my students called me "Master." I got a kick out of this until I noticed none of the Ghanaian teachers were addressed this way. They were called "Sir" or "Madam." This made me uncomfortable so I asked one of the other teachers why I was Master.

"It is because you teach science. It is a more exalted subject than, say, English or history." Then he read my mind and added, "It's not because you are white."

Master or not, my apprehension of the local language hardly improved; Ewe baffled me. My mouth slipped on all but the simplest of greetings and my brain betrayed my best linguistic intentions. I tried to write down words and phrases in the back of my journal but I didn't know how to spell those strings of slurred consonants or vowel sounds that defeated my clumsy tongue. I understood when the hairdresser down the road asked me where I was going each day—one of my only victories—but my vocabulary was limited to "the beach," "the school" and "the post office." (The last hardly counts, since the word for post office in Ewe is *poste*.) If I was headed anywhere else, I retreated into English. The teachers at Three Town scolded my poor Ewe, reminding me that the last Canadian volunteer to work in Denu was a much better student of the language: "By this time Trevor was speaking in sentences and talking to the chief. Marshay, your Ewe is very, very bad."

My biggest gaffe came on a morning when I arrived at the school grounds later than usual. Claire was already teaching her class of sewing students. She paused her lesson to greet me: "Marshay! *Ah li ah?*" which means "Have you arrived?" Ghanaians are fond of stating the obvious. When I shouted back my response, "*Eh ma li*," which I'd learned meant "Yes, I've arrived," Claire and the entire class of girls started laughing and, inexplicably, glanced at my crotch.

Later I found out that instead of telling Claire "Yes, I've arrived" I announced "Yes, I have an erection." The teachers made fun of me for three days afterwards and I worried what new nickname would be born of this.

At eleven years old, Rockson was the youngest of Mr. Quansah's seven sons and my best friend in Denu. We spent Saturday mornings together watching cartoons on the headmaster's television set. Afterwards we played soccer in the schoolyard with his friends and a half-deflated ball. One night Ghana Television broadcast a David Copperfield magic show. After one of Copperfield's first illusions Rockson stood up and looked genuinely repulsed. I asked him what was the matter. "David Copperfield is the Antichrist," he said and walked out of the room.

My favourite day with Rockson came on the Sunday he found the R2-D2 key chain my sister gave me as a going away present.

"What's this?" he asked.

"It's R2D2," I said, and returned to the pile of quizzes I was marking.

"Are too dee too? What does that mean?"

I frowned. "Rockson, you've never heard of *Star Wars*?"

"No. I do not know it."

"You're kidding," I said in ethnocentric shock.

He shook his head. "What is it?"

I pushed away the test papers. "Sit down Rockson. I have a story to tell you. A long time ago, in a galaxy far, far away..."

For the rest of the day I regaled Rockson with a narrative of the *Star Wars* trilogy. As a child of the seventies, I've seen the three films at least a dozen times each, collected all the toys and can pretty much recite each movie word for word. Even my light saber sound effects are well-honed. The adventures of Luke Skywalker and Han Solo are the dominant mythology of my childhood; *Star*

Wars was almost a religion. I remember at Sunday Mass when the priest bid the congregation to offer each other the "sign of peace," my cousins and I would shake hands and say "May the force be with you," which always earned pinches from our parents. Sharing my sci-fi folklore with an eleven-year-old Ghanaian boy was an unexpected joy.

We sat in the living room all afternoon and Rockson was spellbound. He grew excited at the space battles, cheered as Han Solo blasted away Stormtroopers and twice applauded the destruction of the Death Star. I shamelessly hammed up the dialogue by making Luke sound like a whining child and Darth Vader an evil asthmatic. Han Solo, however, always sounded cool.

While some of the technological elements to the story, such as space travel and laser guns, required a bit of explanation, Rockson had a firm grasp of the supernatural. Hairy monsters, Obi-Wan Kenobi's ghost and the Force were concepts that fit easily into his African sensibilities.

"Marcello, what is the Force?"

"It is a magic power the Jedi have. It lets them read minds and move things without touching them—that sort of thing."

"Ah...it is *juju*."

"I guess so."

"Yes. Darth Vader is a *juju* man. A bad one. I understand. The night watchman at the school has strong *juju*, too. Everyone is afraid of him. He is like Darth Vader."

When Mr. Quansah called us to lunch midway through the story we both groaned and Rockson pleaded with me to eat quickly. We finished our meal in record time, returned to the living room, and I revealed to Rockson the secret relationship between Luke Skywalker and Darth Vader.

"And then he said, 'Luke...I am your father.'"

Rockson jumped off his chair. "What? He is lying! That cannot be!"

"That's what Luke said, but then he looked inside of himself and he knew that it was true."

Rockson gasped and shook his head. "I cannot believe it. This is incredible."

It took four hours to get through all three movies. When I reached the end Rockson asked, "Did that really happen?"

"No. It's just a story."

"Are you sure?"

"Pretty sure."

"It is a good story."

"It's my favourite."

I promised to send him the movies on video cassette when I returned to Canada. In the meantime I handed him the R2-D2 key chain.

"May the force be with you."

Near the end of June, as the teachers were getting their mid-term examinations ready, I walked in on a serious meeting in the staff room. A student had fallen ill and wanted to defer his examinations. When I asked the nature of the boy's illness, the teachers all looked at each other for a moment. Then the headmaster spoke.

"I talked to the boy's mother yesterday. She said that three days ago, when the boy returned from school, he was very sick. She took him to the doctor and the doctor examined him. After the examination the doctor said, 'There is nothing wrong with this boy physically. He is spiritually sick.'"

"What does that mean?" I asked.

"It means that somebody has put a curse on him." Mr. Quansah hesitated for a moment, and turned his eyes to the wall. "Apparently, when the boy arrived at one of his classes that day, there was a crumpled leaf on his desk. As soon as he saw the leaf the boy became ill. The boy and his mother believe that one of his enemies went to see a *juju* man who made a spell for him using the leaf. Now the boy is sick."

"This boy is a model student," added Francis, the English teacher. "Before this week his attendance was perfect."

"What will you do about his mid-terms?" I asked.

"We will let him defer. Do not worry about it. He is not one of your biology students. This boy is in form three."

"How long will he be sick?"

"One cannot say. But there are healers who can make him better."

"Really? How does that work?" I asked, fascinated.

"It is okay. Don't worry about it Mr. Marcello. This boy is in form three," the headmaster repeated and the teachers filed out of the staff room without saying another word about it, at least not to me.

As my biology students wrote their own mid-terms, I discovered many shared a less-magical challenge to their academic careers. The exam I composed for my students was a simple one, with test questions drawn directly from the textbook. I didn't want to make the exam too challenging; I wanted my students to do well. The previous year only fourteen percent of students received a passing grade in biology. Idealistic, and naïve, I vowed to change this.

I made up slightly different examinations for each of my four classes and wrote the questions on the blackboard. Each student was to write their answers on a page in their notebooks, then tear out the page and hand it in to me for grading.

On Monday morning of exam week my first class filed into the room. I gave the signal to start and nearly every student began cheating. I watched, stunned, as students leaned across rows to spy on their classmates. Others turned right around in their seats to view the papers behind them, or stood to peer over the shoulders of whoever sat in front. I caught one boy hunting for answers in his textbook. When he realized I was watching, he shook his head, as if to deny any wrongdoing, and waited for me to turn away before resuming his clumsy deception. Outside, students from my other classes peeked through the windows and wrote down the test questions. When I chased them away, the whispering in the classroom reached a roar as students took advantage of my brief distraction to share answers. These were not elegant cheaters.

The following day my other three classes wrote their examinations. Their behaviour was the same. Students who copied the questions from the previous day moaned when they realized I had changed the test, and leaned to steal answers from those beside them. I tried to record the names of the cheaters but I could hardly keep track, and when I took away the papers from those I did catch, they were shocked. Fraud, apparently, is not a crime normally punished in Three Town.

Marking the papers was even more frustrating. Three times I came across a sequence of papers with the exact same answers, right and wrong, with identical spelling mistakes from students who'd sat next to each other during the exam. One enterprising student copied down the questions from the previous class' test, wrote the answers on a separate piece of paper and smuggled it into his own exam. His intention was to hand in the paper already completed with the correct responses. When he saw that I had changed the test he didn't even bother to try to answer the new questions. He handed in the bootlegged paper anyway, knowing that every response was incorrect. I didn't know whether to be angry at his insolence or amused by his ineptitude.

I intended to give a failing grade to each student I caught cheating, but I didn't have to bother; only six out of one hundred and twenty students passed the test. When I showed the results to the head of the science department he was not surprised.

"Very few students ever pass science," he said. "These are not good students. They are lazy. Don't be too concerned."

I felt deflated. I had grand ideas. I thought that with my do-gooder enthusiasm and my "volunteer spirit" I could change things. After the test I understood my arrogance. Why would these students, who never showed any proficiency in science before, suddenly, under the guidance of an untrained teacher, excel? Just because I am from Canada? Just because I wanted them to? I didn't like being humbled.

One of my biology students was named Tristmous. His parents died soon after he was born and he did not remember them. After their death, a family took him in and cared for him until he reached adolescence. "When they found me they did not know what my name was, and they could not ask anybody because my mother and my father were dead. So they named me Tristmous, which means 'the sad one.' It is Latin.

"I have no family in Denu so I must work to pay for my food on my own. I also must go to school so this is very hard for me. But I put my faith in our Lord Jesus Christ. I have prayed to Him, and I believe that He will see that I survive and that I live long. I know that one day I will be an educated man. This is my goal, to become educated. Even though it is difficult for me because I am alone, I know that with the help of Jesus I will not fail. I put my life in His good hands and I know that He will not fail me."

I was touched by Tristmous' story. At fifteen he seemed an old man, and I was astonished at his eloquence and his faith. He had no doubts that his God would deliver him to the life he wanted.

Unfortunately, Tristmous' paper was one of the worst. I doubt he'd ever opened his textbook. When I questioned him he told me he was certain about his education, but instead of studying, he deferred responsibility to Christ.

"With the help of Jesus I will not fail," he told me.

He did fail. Jesus was not marking his test paper; I was. Tristmous' faith did not guarantee his success any more than my good intentions did. I don't know which of the two of us was under the greater delusion.

When I first arrived in Denu everything was unfamiliar; every sensation lacked precedent in memory. It was exhilarating. It is the high that forever addicts a man to strange roads. In one month everything changed. Another feeling, one even more wonderful, took over. All the things that had been alien suddenly became familiar. It seemed to happen overnight. Aromas that once made me cautious made me hungry. I knew which woman in the marketplace sold the best pineapples and I bought them from her nearly every day. I had a favourite roadside bar where I bought my favourite local beer. I knew a shortcut to the beach some of the locals didn't know. Nobody told me how at home I'd feel. They never mentioned this in my orientation.

But the first child of comfort is tedium. As my days became more and more routine there were times I felt bored. There was little to do in Denu after school let out; there are only so many lonely beers a man can drink, so many novels to read in the school library, and so many games of soccer to play with eleven-year-old boys. For all its slow-moving charms village life lacked excitement. I longed for easy English conversations, nightlife, Western music. I craved my old familiar.

A long weekend followed the mid-term examinations and I took the opportunity to travel to Asawinso, Anne's village. I didn't know how to reach Asawinso—it was a distant speck on my map and nobody in Denu had ever heard of the place—so I travelled into Accra to find transport.

The CNB Motor Park in Accra was a sprawling circus of noise, humanity and automobiles. Scattered amid shady trees and mud were hundreds of vehicles, mostly minibuses and *tro-tro*s, destined for the countless towns and villages that lie north and east of the capital. Drivers shouted out destinations like machine-gun fire: "Takoraditakoraditakoradi!" Luggage handlers deftly plucked my pack from my shoulder before knowing where I was headed. Young girls with soft voices sold cold water in tiny plastic bags, while boys peddling underwear, batteries and frozen yogourt, blew me kisses to get my attention. Preachers looked for an audience and chickens pecked at trash. Beggars—either singing blind men led by dutiful grandchildren or lonely withered women—patrolled the park with open palms. Stereos blasted highlife music loud enough to overcome the noise of crowds and backfiring engines. Women sold slices of pineapple or handfuls of boiled groundnuts from trays balanced impossibly on their heads. Smells told of frying yams and diesel fumes.

A man in a blue booth sold me a ticket to Cape Coast, a city halfway between Accra and Asawinso where I would spend the night.

"Go there," the man said, pointing to a vehicle a few metres away. "Under the big tree." Then began the friendly struggle with the *mate*, the driver's assistant. He demanded a bogus baggage fee, a tax levied only on foreigners who don't know better.

"You pay me one thousand *cedis* for your bag."

"No, I will not. There is no fee for luggage."

"Okay then, you pay me five hundred."

"I will give you nothing. Nobody else pays you for their bags."

"Yes, everybody does."

"Then I will watch, and when I see another person give you money, I will pay you also."

"No, no my friend. You must pay me something, or else I will not put your bag on the roof."

"Then I will do it myself."

"Go ahead if you like."

The man thought I was bluffing—after all everyone knows white men don't do such things—but I swung my bag onto my back and climbed the metal ladder on the back of the *tro-tro*. People began to gather around; a *yavu* on the roof of a *tro-tro* is quite a spectacle. I secured my pack onto the pile like I had seen done dozens of times and the small crowd cheered. Another passenger came up to the car and looked up at me with some confusion. I gestured for him to pass me his bag. The man turned to the *mate* who shrugged and said, "Give it to him. Mr. America wants to work today."

As my *tro-tro* was about to leave the motor park, a blind preacher in white robes came aboard. He had no seat but stood instead at the front of the vehicle and faced us. As soon as our vehicle reached the highway the preacher began his service by leading the passengers in prayer. A woman seated next to me jabbed an elbow into my ribs and whispered, "Bow your head. We are praying to God." The holy man pulled out a large copy of the Gospel of Luke written in Braille. Every passenger was mesmerized as his fingers brushed across invisible words and his voice spoke scripture over the clatter of a dying engine. After the reading he began his sermon, an instruction on how to avoid sin and achieve salvation. He smiled as he spoke and his sightless eyes seemed fixed on something no one else could see. This man was different from the other preachers I had seen who shouted prayers at the sky and at passersby loud enough for God to hear. He was all softness, serenity and beauty. When he finished, he led us in prayer one more time and collected coin donations from his congregation. He was let out on the side of the road, alone, with his Braille Bible.

I arrived in Cape Coast minutes before the start of an awesome rainstorm that overflowed open sewers, turning the streets into a brown river. I had never seen rain fall so deliberately. I waded through the knee-high muck to my hotel, at times nearly being washed off my feet. The flood smelled mildly of sewage and the rain added a stickiness to the air. Two boys followed me back to my hotel carrying an umbrella over my head and tried, like good hosts, to ensure my head stayed dry even though the rest of me was soaked.

The next morning meant another motor park and another wait for a *tro-tro*, but I couldn't find a driver who knew how to get to Asawinso. No one had even heard of it. The consensus was that I could not reach it from Cape Coast, and they directed me north to Kumasi to find a vehicle.

The ride to Kumasi saw a different diversion. Instead of a preacher, our *tro-tro* was boarded by a man selling an herbal cure-all medicine. He, too, began by leading us in prayer and I bowed my head obediently for fear of sore ribs. The salesman followed the prayer with an animated recollection of the terrible physical ailments he once endured. He stood at the front of the bus, bent over and gripping his back. Making sloppy mock diarrhea noises, he mimed the flow of filth that once exited his body via a diseased colon for his captive audience. While he continued his pathogenic pantomime, photographs were passed around the bus depicting victims of other gruesome ailments. There were richly coloured photographs of a child whose face was covered with strange blisters, a man whose genitals were swollen to the size of melons, and the back view of a poor boy squatting over the pool of blood just spurted from his bowels. The grisly photos were in stark contrast to the salesman whose antics had the energetic humour of a circus clown. It was strange to see an audience bent and laughing while viewing pictures of people crippled with ghastly disease.

The sales pitch was finely polished and peppered with self-deprecating humour that the passengers swallowed like honey:

> *You may say that I talk too loud!*
> *You may say that my mouth is too wide!*
> *You may say that I eat too much of the* fufu!
> *You may say that my belly is too much round!*
> *I may be a noisy man!*
> *I may be a fat man!*
> *I may be impossible!*
> *Intolerable!*
> *Irrepressible!*
> *Inexcusable!*
> *But I know the cure and I want to share the cure with you!*

He passed around "the cure" for us to sample. It was a reddish liquid contained in a tiny vial. Our salesman urged us to rub a bit of the liquid on our temples, forehead and chest to enjoy its natural healing properties. Everyone did this and soon the bus stunk of black licorice and nail-polish remover. Once he finished his pitch he asked if anyone would like to purchase the miracle medicine. Every hand waved cash. He sold his entire inventory and handed out instruction booklets in both English and Twi. Like the other salesman, the preacher, he was let out at the side of the highway.

I arrived in Asawinso after dark. Anne was thrilled to see me; her placement was not going well. She taught elementary mathematics to seven-year-old students who understood little English. Further, she was expected to dole out corporal punishment when they misbehaved. She refused to do this, even though she was provided with a stick for this purpose. Once her students realized the new teacher would not hit them, they felt free to misbehave. Anne could not control them.

But it was her relationship with her host family that gave Anne the most stress. Her host father was a minister at a local church. Each Sunday he brought Anne to the service and sat her at the front of the church to face the congregation. He showed off his Canadian charge to the village, boasting that he had a white woman under his care. Anne did not know how to react and considered changing her placement to another family.

She needed a vacation. We jumped the pre-dawn bus to Kumasi, the nearest major city, and swam in a chic hotel pool. "This is cheating," she said, as we sat on the pool deck drinking Heineken and eating pizza, denying Africa for an afternoon.

Later that day we travelled south to Accra, where we spent the weekend dancing. We went to Piccadilly Circle, a bar filled with prostitutes and spilled beer, where waiters in ironic bow ties tried to lend some class to the squalor. Anne and I danced together, apart, alone and with every man or woman who wanted to teach us dance steps and sell us drugs or sex.

"Move your hips like this now."

"Now bend your knees a little."

"That is it."

"You got it now."

"Is that your wife?"

"You want to smoke good wee?"

Good Vibrations played highlife and reggae tunes all night, and we got drunk on cheap beer and the Accra nightlife. While we caught our breath at a table, our waiter informed us that prostitutes identify themselves in Accra bars by smoking. Anne butted out her cigarette and we returned to the dance floor.

I never danced at home; it was something that I never wanted to do. It took a night at Piccadilly to finally move me. My my feet still recall the steps that changed me, and I can still hear the music in my head.

Anne and I danced until the sun peered out over the open air dance floor and chased us out. Laughing and breathless, we passed the omelet stands, cigarette vendors and drug dealers and made our way "home" to tiny hotel beds.

The weekend ended too quickly, and I returned to Denu before I had my fill of late nights, sweaty nightclubs and jammed *tro-tro*s.

I remembered a few weeks before when I spent a weekend in Accra, in search of distractions. Following the advice of my guide-book, I checked into a hotel frequented by foreigners. I befriended a group of American Peace Corps volunteers who invited me along for some Western-style diversions. In the Osu district of Accra, home of much of the city's expat population, we visited O'Ryan's Irish Pub. There, bored development workers and foreign businessmen shot pool while drinking overpriced Guiness. The stereo played non-descript fiddle music at deafening volumes. The only African was the bartender. He was wearing an ill-fitting tuxe-do shirt and a green bow tie and didn't smile much.

We couldn't find a table at O'Ryan's so we took a cab to a Mexican sports bar on the other side of town. Under giant television screens flashing with ESPN, we drank Coronas and ate burritos that, because of the insane air conditioning, got cold quickly. A stereo blasted American classic rock. The volunteers and I talked a bit about music and travelling, but mostly they discussed how lazy Ghanaians were and how anxious they were to return to the United States. An obnoxious Australian joined us and bought a round of beers and chicken wings. "Courtesy of the World Bank," he boast-ed as he flipped me his business card.

As we left the bar, a skeletal prostitute wearing little more than rags called out to us. She reduced her prices when we declined her services, trying to bargain away her body to white men as we looked for a cab.

I returned to Denu the next morning, a day earlier than planned. It was pouring rain when I stepped out of my *tro-tro* at the Denu-Aflao junction. I started to walk down the main road when a man on a bicycle rode up to me.

"The rain is beating you," he said. "You can ride with me." I sat on the rack behind the seat and he pedalled me to the school.

"Thank you," I said. We were both soaked.

"Don't mention."

The rain had ended in time to kick a ball around with Rockson and his friends. It felt good to be home.

But the African nightlife on this trip to the capital with Anne was intoxicating, wild and welcoming; far more real than the misplaced Irish Pubs that centred on homesick and jaded Westerners. I vowed to spend my time in Africa with Africans. If I wanted phony Irish Pubs I could have stayed in Calgary where they grow like weeds.

As I walked to the school on Tuesday, my legs still weary from dancing, there was a new sign on the school bulletin board:

Pork Show!!
The sale of Three Town pork is rescheduled to come off
Sunday July 6
Come early to avoid disappointment.
It is a good lean meat.
No credit.

As part of their agricultural science program senior male students at Three Town had to learn to raise and tend pigs. At the end of the semester, one unfortunate swine is slaughtered and sold to raise money for the school coffers.

The sale was a much anticipated event in Denu as pork is considered something of a luxury meat. Never having attended a pork show before I arrived early, to avoid disappointment. The scene was a cross between a carnival and a William Golding nightmare. The carcass was laid on the ground under some shade and sliced into sloppy pieces by the proud students. One boy sawed into the carcass while others slapped the bits of meat, skin and organs into neat piles on a large sheet of plastic. Potential customers browsed the steaming piles of pig looking for the wet heap that seemed to be the best bargain. Often customers had to wave away a layer of meat-crazed flies that settled on the raw swine. The smell was incredible. After a customer chose his pork, one of the students rushed to scoop up the mound of meat and guts with both hands and dump it into a small plastic bag. Money was exchanged. Everyone was happy.

It was an exciting event, and it wasn't long before all the pork was sold. All the while, the luckless pig's head laid on its side in a corner of the yard, staring at the commotion through a cloud of flies.

The pork show was the start of an eventful week at Three Town. On the following Friday, the student social committee held one of their regular Film Days. Two Fridays each semester the students gathered to watch a movie on video instead of attending their regular classes. The entire student population crammed into a single classroom, covered up the windows to keep out the light—and fresh oxygen—and stared at whatever might be flickering on the screen. Two hours later everybody streamed out of the suffocating room, drenched in sweat and blinking in the sunlight. It was great fun.

This Film Day was marred with controversy. There was serious disagreement as to what the selected film should be. Two of the student organizers requested a film called *Bitter Love*, a Nigerienne-made romance. The assistant headmaster was enraged at the suggestion.

"*Bitter Love*? Why does everything have to be about your organs? Everyone wants to see movies about love and organs. That is all you people are concerned about! There will be no *Bitter Love* at this school. No organs! No organs!"

Instead the students saw *Diablo 3*, the third installment in a series of popular Ghanaian films about a boy who turns into a snake. The premise was simple. A greedy woman who sells stew in the marketplace wants to increase her profits. She enlists the help of the village *juju* priest who conjures up a spell using a lock of hair from the woman's son. Her stew is magically irresistible and people line up for hours to buy a bowl.

There is a catch. The *juju* man warns the woman never to serve any of her magic stew to her son otherwise he will suffer a terrible curse. But the woman is careless and leaves a pot in the kitchen unattended. The boy returns from school hungry, sees the stew and serves himself a big bowl. After an eternity of groaning, screaming and frothing at the mouth, the boy collapses to the floor and turns into a snake. Meanwhile, the mother senses her error and rushes home in a panic—tripping and crying all the way. Alas, she is too late and is promptly strangled to death by her serpent son.

The remainder of the film follows the boy around as he continually morphs to and from his slithery alter ego and murders whoever might be in the room. The authorities pursue snake-boy, but every time they lock him up, he turns into a snake and slithers to freedom between the bars of his jail cell.

The film was a hit. Even students who campaigned for *Bitter Love* felt that *Diablo 3* was a good compromise, although many wondered why no one in the film ever tries to kill the snake. The assistant headmaster was relieved there were no organs in the film, Freudian analyses aside.

Although the film was silly and the classroom theatre uncomfortable, Film Day was a fun and popular occasion. Nothing, though, could have prepared me for the next event that marked the end of the semester.

It was sunny when about thirty students gathered in the schoolyard during the lunch break. They met the school chaplain, who came out of his office with a long stick and a list of students accused of misbehaving. Grinning, the chaplain walked into the centre of the crowd and scanned the faces of the condemned. Most students shuddered and moved out of reach of his stick, while a few brave others stepped forward, hoping to be first to get the whole ordeal over with. Finally the chaplain nodded to one frightened girl and the rest of the students hooted and cheered. She stepped forward and nervously extended her upturned hand. The chaplain raised the reed over his head and brought it down with a whistling smack on the girl's palm. The crowd cheered again. She winced and rubbed her palm against her thigh before extending it again. *Whack*! She shook her hand in pain and held it out one more time. *Whack!* The crowd applauded and the girl sulked away, blowing on her hand. Then the chaplain turned his stick to each of the others on his list.

I was strapped once in junior high school. I'd fooled around in religion class, a serious crime at St. Helena, and was sent to the office. There, my giant-headed vice principal drew a leather strap from his top desk drawer. "You have to learn some respect," he said. I'd pleaded for clemency but the leather bit the back of my hand five times. I was humiliated. At the bus stop after school I jammed my hand in my pocket to hide the red welts. My friends asked me if I cried. I told them no, but I'm sure my eyes betrayed me.

But as the minor terror continued at Three Town, everyone remained in good spirits. The happy violence seemed more a social event than a punishment as each strike of the chaplain's stick was met with cheers. Onlookers applauded students who tried to dupe the chaplain by switching hands between blows, even though this tactic always failed. Some of the older students, especially the boys, tried hard not to show any pain or emotion during their caning. These heroes drew the most laughter as even the most stoic couldn't help but moan after three hard whacks. Not a single student objected to their punishment. There were no pleas for last minute pardons from the chaplain, there was no anger and no tears. Some students laughed even as their own hands were struck. The weird music of slaps, squeals and cheers filled the schoolyard until all the condemned met their fate and returned to their classrooms. Everyone was smiling, even those with hot reddened palms. I couldn't believe it. For them caning was nothing tragic.

I fell in love with the food in Ghana. I loved the street-side stalls that served fantastic omelet sandwiches, hot yams with *palava*, and bowls of Red-Red: red beans and rice cooked in red palm oil. I loved boiled groundnuts and the orange tiger nuts that tasted a little like Captain Crunch. I couldn't get enough slimy okra stew, dubbed "snot soup" by some volunteers, and I enjoyed the kebabs sold at the Denu-Aflao junction so much I stopped worrying what meat they were made of. I learned that *shito*, despite its name, is a tasty hot sauce that leaves the tongue burning happily. I discovered the best way to cool a *shito*-scorched palate is with an ice cold bottle of "Pee Cola." I nearly choked on my first swallow of *fufu* but I quickly learned to love and crave it. I avoided Denu's cat soup vendor, but in Kumasi I ate a bowl of bush rat stew. It was delicious.

The best food, though, came from my host mother's kitchen. My enthusiasm for her cooking pleased her, and when my volunteer placement neared its end, she strived to find new things for me to try. Most nights, though, we dined on fish soup with *banku*, a fermented corn mash that managed, impossibly, to be sour and tasty. I never mastered eating with my fingers, but my sticky-to-the-wrist right hand and soup-splattered shirts provided my family with enough entertainment to forgive my messiness.

My host family asked me about the kinds of food I ate in Canada, and Rockson was disappointed to hear there was no *banku* in Calgary. "Then I will never come to visit you," he said sadly. One weekend I decided to prepare a typical meal for them: pasta with tomato sauce. The kind of sauce my grandmother taught me to make. I was sure they would love it.

Aside from fresh tomatoes and onions, the Denu market did not have the ingredients I needed, so I left the country. According to my guidebook there was a Western-style supermarket in Lomé, the capital city in neighbouring Togo. I grabbed my passport and took a taxi to the border. I waited in line for a half hour at the customs post while officials examined my visa, then found a money-changer who converted my Ghanaian *cedis* into West African *francs*. I wondered if anyone had gone through this sort of effort for tomato sauce before—it was the most involved grocery run of my life. My grandmother would have been proud.

After fifteen minutes on the back of a motorcycle taxi I reached the supermarket in downtown Lomé. Inside, the aggressively air-conditioned store looked like every other supermarket I'd ever seen, and after spending nearly three months buying food from street vendors, it was almost alien. The shelves were neat and orderly and stocked with expensive imported goods, mostly from France. I almost bought a pound of dark-roasted coffee beans until I realized I had no way to brew them. I found a bottle of extra virgin olive oil, some dried rotini, and a small bag of Italian herbs. In the produce aisle I picked up a withered bulb of garlic, and to my joy, a bag of fresh oyster mushrooms.

I returned home after another hour or so of going backwards through customs officials, money-changers and taxi drivers. I strutted into the kitchen and unloaded my treasures. (I put one mushroom aside for my biology students. They were studying a unit on taxonomy, and when I taught about Kingdom Fungi, nobody knew what I was talking about.) Mr. Quansah, his wife and several of their sons crowded around to observe my work. One of the boys, named God's Way, sat with a pen poised on a scrap of paper to record the recipe.

I chopped the onion and tomatoes and dropped a few slivers of garlic into some hot oil. When the aroma hit my nose I swooned. The sound and smell of garlic sizzling in olive oil stirred my latent Italian sensibilities. I added the mushrooms and spices to the mix and stood over the pot to breathe in the fragrant steam. Then I tossed in the tomatoes and let the sauce simmer gloriously.

While I enjoyed these moments of garlicky nostalgia there was some concern on the part of my audience.

"Where is the meat?" my host mother asked.

"There is none. I'm using these mushrooms instead."

"Oh." A pause. "Are you sure you do not need any meat for this?"

"I'm pretty sure."

Another pause. "But could you put meat in the sauce if you wanted to?"

"Yes, of course. Whatever you like."

She seemed relieved. "Good. That is good."

When the sauce was finished, I spooned it out onto some noodles and served it to the crowd. Everyone was enthusiastic at first, but after a few bites I could tell they were not impressed.

"What is this?" Kwashie asked, pointing to a bit of green on his plate.

"That's oregano. It's an herb."

"Ah," he replied, pushing it aside. "So this is Canadian food?"

"Not really. It's Italian food. This is the kind of food my family eats."

"And there is never any meat in it?"

They picked politely at their pasta, looking up at me with forced smiles.

"This is very good," God's Way said, charmingly insincere. "You are a very good cook." The reviews were lukewarm but I hardly noticed; I was too busy enjoying the meal. I finished my pasta in record time and eyed the half-finished plates of the others who were suddenly "full."

One of the other Crossroads volunteers, Melanie, kept a list of everything she missed about Canada. She added to it daily, and it included everything from red wine to oral sex. I thought this was ridiculous. We had been in Ghana for less than two months and I don't think there was anything I really longed for. But tasting that pasta sauce with the familiar basil, oregano and garlic aroused my first pangs of homesickness. Ghanaian cuisine was wild and wonderful, but I truly missed my food.

Afia walked into the house as I finished everyone's leftovers. She was the home science teacher who taught cooking at the school. Afia looked down at my plate and scowled.

"What is this you are eating?"

"Marshay-Marshay cooked for us," one of the children said. "It is Italy food."

I gave her a spoonful. "It is just pepper-less gravy," she declared, handing me back my spoon. "And you forgot to put in the meat."

My host family never asked me to cook again, and I knew the bottle of olive oil would sit unused on their countertop for months. In truth, I didn't care. The smell of garlic lingered on my fingertips for two days. I brought them to my nose and smelled home.

With each new experience in Ghana I felt a crack of internal growth. It happened slowly, haltingly, in the passing days and moments of reflection. Home and who I was wasn't being forgotten as much as it was shifting in my mind. This is the gift of distance. Still, even as I slipped further from my old world, I found that it could always crash back into me and change me into my old self again.

One evening Mom called.

"I have bad news," she said. "Are you sitting down?"

"Don't be so dramatic, Mom. What's going on?"

"Dad and I are breaking up."

There had been another fight. Dad got drunk and hit one of my sisters, Sabrina. Then he hit my mom. After twenty-five years with him, this hardly qualified as news. But this time was the worst. This time I wasn't there to stop him and this time he banged up Mom and my sister pretty bad. This time the police came and took Dad away.

"Are you okay?" I asked.

Mom was crying. "Yeah."

"And Sabrina?"

"She's fine. Everyone's been really supportive. Your dad's a mess. He doesn't have anyone."

"That's his own fault."

"I guess." She paused. "How are you? What do you think?"

"I don't know. I'm sorry I wasn't there."

"I'm glad you weren't here. There was nothing you could have done."

"Yes, there was. I would have stopped him."

"You might have made things worse."

She was right. When it comes to my father I am no diplomat. The police might have carted both of us away, or maybe just me.

"Is it over now?" I asked.

"Yes."

"Are you sure? This has happened before."

"Not like this. It is over. I'm sorry."

"What are you sorry for?"

"I don't know."

"Do you want me to come home?"

She thought for a moment. "No. We'll be all right. Everyone's been really supportive."

We talked a little while longer. When I hung up Mr. Quansah could see that something was wrong.

"Is everything all right in Canada?" he asked.

I told him what happened. I told him about my father, his alcoholism, and the years of abuse. My blood grew hot. I told Mr. Quansah things I'd never told anyone and this was selfish because he didn't understand. Divorce and domestic violence was as alien to him as cat soup was to me. He looked at the wall, sometimes nodding, sometimes shifting in his chair. But I was shaking with anger, and I didn't care if he felt uncomfortable because at that moment, he was all I had. I could either talk to him or go outside and scream and wake the whole fucking village.

I was exhausted by the time I ran out of words. We both were. I stood to go to sleep and tried to apologize but Mr. Quansah shook his head.

"No, no. It is okay. Tomorrow you will feel better." I shook his hand, snapped my fingers against his and went to my room.

Two days before I left Calgary I had a fight with my dad. In anger I told him going to Africa was my way to get away from him. At the airport he cried as if he wasn't going to see me again. Maybe he was right. I lay in bed as if at home, as if I were twelve years old, fists hard and sweating after one of my parents' fights. I can get older, I can cross oceans, but there are things I cannot get away from.

One night a few weeks later as I walked home from Hotel Vilcabamba, I heard drumming and singing penetrate the dark. I followed it into a side street when I felt a hand touch mine. I turned to see a young girl I'd never met. She was about ten years old and wore a pretty white dress. Her tightly braided hair was decorated with red and yellow beads. She spoke to me in Ewe. When she realized I didn't understand she giggled, shook her head and held my hand. She led me down a dark road to a large walled compound. She pushed open the gate and gestured for me to enter.

Inside, a circle of benches outlined a dance floor where about thirty villagers were singing, dancing and drumming in the light of a full moon. When they saw me enter they waved me forward and invited me to sit.

"We do this every night," a man said to me. "You are welcome."

I kicked up cool night sand with bare feet while a village watched and cheered and clapped. I'd never danced like this before, if I'd ever danced at all. I sang songs I didn't understand and proclaimed words of love I could not pronounce. Every night afterwards I danced, drummed and sweated with those wonderful people. In those moments I was no longer a stranger. I was not the *yavu* who taught at the secondary school. I was a brother with a cowry-shell rattle clacking in time in darkness.

That was the miracle, the most impossible thing of all: *I* was a part of that glorious noise. *My* arms flapped to drum beats, *my* feet shuffled across circles in the dust, *my* eyes closed as if I were swimming. Looking back I can scarcely understand how they could be *my* eyes and *my* arms? Did a small African girl smile at me, bring me here and wipe the sweat from my face with white cloth? Did my hands hold sticks and beat goat skin? What were the songs in my head I could not understand and how could such pulsing ancient joy be mine? Why was my bed just across the path and not an ocean away?

My face does not betray that I have done such things. Sometimes I wish it did. I wish that its boldness could change. I wish my eyes would shine with my experiences so anyone who saw me could tell I know a place where I learned to dance and drum and sing to strange music. I want people to see the miracle in my eyes.

The school year ended in August, my students had finished writing their final examinations, and I was free to leave Denu. I decided to lighten my pack. I took a pocket knife to my guidebook and cut away chapters on countries I would not visit. The St. Christopher medallion my mother gave me before I left Canada ended up around my host mother's neck, along with a *pagna* of silky white cloth I bought her. I bought Rockson a new soccer ball and gave him most of my T-shirts; they had been slowly replaced with colourful African shirts. I gave the teachers my Canadian flag necklace and a bag of Canada pins. The school library took my heaviest item, a copy of Umberto Eco's *The Island of the Day Before*.

On my last day at the school, the staff held a farewell party in the staff room for me, complete with beer, plates of salad and fried guinea fowl prepared by Claire's home science students. While everybody filled their plates Mr. Quansah made a speech in my honour:

"When Mr. Marcello first arrived here three months ago I said to myself, 'How can this man be a good teacher? He is so small.' But this little man from Canada exceeded my expectations and proved to be a fine addition to our staff. We are sad to see him leave. But Mr. Marcello is an adventurer. He wants to see all of Africa, but we know that he will like Ghana best of all. We wish him a safe journey and hope he will return to visit us soon." The teachers applauded and the headmaster handed me a white plastic bag. "On behalf of your fellow teachers here at Three Town, I give you this gift so that you never forget your friends in Denu."

Inside the bag was a shirt and trouser set made of green and burgundy tie-dyed cloth. Elegant gold embroidery swirled around the collar, cuffs and sleeves. In my three months in Africa I had never seen such beautiful clothes, and I struggled against tears.

"You can wear this in Canada, and everyone will be jealous," Afia shouted and everybody laughed. The crowd urged me to try on the clothes. The shirt fit me perfectly but the trousers were huge; the waistband reached the top of my chest.

"Two *yavu* could fit in these," I said and everyone laughed again.

I rolled down the waistband until my feet appeared from the cuffs and posed for a photo with the other teachers. I was the only one wearing African clothes. Then I stepped forward to address my friends. I thanked them for their kind words, hospitality and friendship. I promised I would never forget my time in Denu. My speech was short. And trite. And clichéd. I wanted to say so much more. I wanted to tell them how much I would miss gossiping with the home science teachers, how I'd miss the dust of the science lab, the chalk on my hands. I wanted to apologize for being a poor teacher, in spite of their accolades. I wanted to tell them how much I loved them. I wanted to tell them that when I thought about how much I learned and unlearned, and when I realized all I'd given back were lessons in biology, I felt like a thief.

I didn't say any of this because I was afraid I'd start to cry. The next morning I would start travelling alone through West Africa. I didn't want to seem soft.

After the party, I needed to be alone to calm my emotions—or at least to hide them. I stepped out for a walk around the campus. Swampland bordered the schoolyard. It extended behind the pens where the agri-science students kept their pigs. Standing there, surrounded by dusk, I watched as a thousand dragonflies rose out of the swamp like a whirlwind. A flock of sparrows met them in the space between the math rooms and the vacant building where boys played table tennis after school.

In a frenzy the birds darted in and out of the swarm, snatching bugs from mid-air. The sky in the schoolyard became thick with motion and the noise of flapping sparrows, the buzz of dragonfly wings and the crunch of bugs in beaks. The sunset smeared a red backdrop for this wild dance.

It wasn't enough to stand on the edges and watch this winged meteor shower. I had to step inside it. I held my breath as birds nearly collided with my head. Dragonflies, clumsier, bounced off my back and chest. I felt the breezes they made as they somersaulted in the air and clouded the horizon. I felt courageous and free. I felt like I could do anything.

Ghana: Travelling

I sat, crushed, in the back of a jammed bush taxi headed west. Next to me was a woman with her two-year-old son on her lap. As we bounced along the highway he looked up at her and said something in Hausa. The mother gave him a disapproving look and called out to the driver to pull the taxi over. The other passengers emitted a collective groan. The woman picked up her son and gave him to the man seated in front of us. The child was handed from passenger to passenger until he reached the man in the front window seat. The last man pulled down the child's trousers and held him outside the open window. The boy held his legs aloft and pissed on the ground. When he was finished the man brought him back inside the window and passed him back to his mother. The driver revved the engine and we were on our way again.

The little boy never said a word. His expression didn't even change. But what is more amazing is I almost didn't write this down. It seemed too ordinary.

Leaving Denu I made my way to Accra where I spent a couple of days at the Hotel California, my favourite Accra hotel. Each time I had gone to Accra—whether it was to exchange money, obtain visas for further travel, or to feel the pulse and noise of the big city—I'd stayed at the Hotel California.

The place was a dive. The rooms were stuffy, the pillows smelly and the mosquitoes oppressive. High-speed ceiling fans swayed dangerously when switched on, and looked ready to crash down and purée me as I slept. The few shared bathrooms were kept clean, but one of the two hotel showers was in the courtyard and any second-storey window had an unobstructed view of whoever was showering below. Some of the doors looked as if they'd been recently kicked in, but potential thieves need not exert themselves. On one visit my neighbour locked himself out and we discovered that each guest key opened the door to every room in the hotel.

What Hotel California lacked in amenities and security it made up in sleazy charm, and its name ensured it was always full of Western tourists wisecracking about "pink champagne on ice." In turn, the tourists attracted a crowd of local hustlers and hangers-on who came to meet, or scam, naïve foreigners. At night, California's sprawling patio was a circus of *djembe*-toting Rastafarians and backpackers donning varying degrees of sunburn.

I arrived from Denu on a Thursday night and the patio was jammed. The stereo punched out music from pirated Alpha Blondy and Yellow Man cassettes. The aggressive reggae drowned out, mercifully, noise from the sofa where a Ghanaian teenager gave drum lessons to a pair of rhythmless Americans. In the lobby, an over-muscled Englishman talked on the phone with his girlfriend in Peru. A Japanese couple waved at the waitress to bring them their change. She pretended not to notice. An Australian spilled his beer on his *Lonely Planet*. Nearby, "Rasta John" instructed a very white German on the fine art of dreadlocking.

"You want to make the dreads you have to liberate yourself from the comb. Understand? This is what you do, liberate yourself from the comb." Rasta John held his hand up. "You see this? This is your new comb. Only your hand you use for your hair.

"Next thing. You have to wash your hair with no shampoo. Understand? No soap or anything. Okay? You must take a leaf and rub it on your hair, okay? No soap. And when your hair is wet you must rub it with leaf—"

"Wait a minute, I have to rub a leaf on my head?"

"Yes. No shampoo. Only leaf."

"What kind of leaf?"

"You know...leaf from tree."

"Yes, but the trees in Germany are different from the trees in Ghana."

"Any leaf is good. No problem."

The biggest crowd, however, was around Romantic Bombastic, Hotel California's shirtless, dreadlocked monarch. He was not a guest or employee of the hotel, but every time I'd visited he was there, drinking beer, smoking cigarettes and chatting with the mob. A gaunt Ghanaian woman acted as Romantic's queen and cardinal attendant. She sat on the chair behind him, her hand on his shoulder and left only when he sent her off to prepare his meals. I never heard her speak. Rounding out Romantic's court was his pet "bush cat," a weird weasel-like animal he kept in a tiny wire globe. The bush cat, who had no name, was only slightly smaller than his cage and constantly circled his prison looking for an escape. The three of them—one gregarious, the other two, silent and nameless—made for a strange royal family.

Romantic was talking about his hotel plans again. He claimed he was building a hotel on the beach east of Accra, though this seemed an unlikely venture for a man who didn't own a shirt.

"I have land on the beach," he said to a collection of attentive travellers. "It is very beautiful. And on the land there is two hills. I will build the hotel on one of the hills, and the other hill I will take a bulldozer and make it flat. Then I put in a zoo with animals and a restaurant that serves European food. And the beach will be very beautiful. Tourists will come and they will love it.

"But one thing: There are villages on the beach, next to my land. And the people have no school, no education, and they come to the beach and shit in the water. It is a big problem for me. Who will want to come to my beach if there is shit all over the place? On the beach and in the water? It is disgusting, all this shit. I tell them. I say, 'Don't shit in the water! Go to shit somewhere else!' But they do not listen. They are poor and ignorant people. They do not know that if there is shit on the beach the tourists would not come. So they will have to shit somewhere else after my hotel is built, because the tourists they do not like the shit."

I asked Romantic why I always saw him on the patio. "Shouldn't you be working on your hotel?"

"I am waiting for my bulldozers to come—from France."

Two Aussies stepped in from the street holding banana leaves filled with sweet-smelling rice and stew. The mass of hungry travellers grew excited. "Where did you get that?" someone asked.

"From some ladies at the end of the street. They've got bowls of this stuff, with chicken and rice and sauce. It's fantastic. And right cheap."

A half dozen backpackers rose to seek out the rice-and-sauce lady, but Romantic protested. "You don't want to eat that. No, no, no. They make that with chicken and all day long the chicken walks in the sewers and eats shit. It is true. You can see them. The chickens eat shit and then you eat the chickens? It is no good. You are eating shit. If you want, she will make you something." He pointed to his girlfriend behind him, but the crowd was already out the gate. Romantic shrugged and dragged on his cigarette.

I moved over to the next table and met two pretty Dutch girls, Deidre and Marie. They were complaining about Africa.

"I am so tired. I want to go home," Deidre said. "The African men are driving me crazy. In Mali it was the worst. Especially Mopti. They were like mosquitoes. Are you going there? It is like hell."

Marie nodded her agreement. "And the anti-malaria pills are making me sick. I am sick of having crazy dreams. It's weird stuff every night. Look at my skin; I've been in Africa for two months and I have no tan. My skin is white, white, white. It is the fucking mefloquine pills. They are keeping me from tanning. When I go back to Holland my friends are going to laugh at me."

Deidre finished her beer. "We are going to get some hamburgers and then go see a movie," she said. "Do you want to come?"

"No. I'm not homesick enough for Ghanaian burgers."

"You will be," Marie warned and they left the patio.

I woke the next morning feeling sick. My mouth was pasty and my head throbbed. I sat and pressed my palm to my forehead. *Is it a fever?* I wondered. *Oh God.*

I reached into my pack and pulled out my guidebook. *Do my joints ache?* I opened the section on travel health and matched my symptoms to the diseases listed. Headaches and fever matched malaria. I dragged my fingers over my body in search of mosquito bites. There were three on my feet. *I should have worn my boots last night.* I kept reading and found I might also have typhoid, hepatitis, or yellow fever. *Is my neck stiff?* I tried to touch my ears to my shoulders. *Oh God. Maybe I have meningitis.*

I took a mental inventory of meals I'd had the day before; I could have had food poisoning, I reasoned. Breakfast: an omelet sandwich and a cup of Milo. The chef cooked it fresh in front of me and used boiled water for the Milo. It was probably safe. Lunch: garden egg stew at the motor park, and a bottle of water. The stew tasted fine and there was no meat in it. It could have been spoiled, though. *Was the seal on the water bottle broken?* I couldn't remember. Dinner: bread and kebabs at Afrikiko. I was sure the meat was cooked through and I'd eaten there before. Then a Fanta, two big beers at the hotel, and two more at The Piccadilly. No, maybe it was three more beers.

Five beers. I didn't have typhoid, I had a hangover. I knew the headache felt familiar. I pulled on a shirt, swallowed three Tylenol and bought an omelet sandwich.

I wandered in Accra for a couple of days then paid a visit to Richard, the Crossroads volunteer coordinator. He told me the paramount chief of Cape Coast was dead. I took a *tro-tro* into town to join the thousands of mourners who gathered to celebrate his funeral. The streets were a frenzy.

Chiefs from around West Africa came to honour the deceased with gifts and song. All day they walked slowly along Intin Road under giant umbrellas. Most chiefs wore red and black robes, traditional colours for Ghanaian funerals. Others wore lengths of garish *kente* cloth, heavy gold jewellery and Rolex watches. An entourage of servants and devotees followed each chief. Drums the size of tree trunks, some draped in coloured cloth, balanced sideways on the heads of servant boys. Shirtless drummers followed, their hands a blur, beating a million rhythms on the high vertical skins. Teenage boys carried carved wooden stools and thrones, baskets and large wooden chests. I saw a trio of young girls carrying ceremonial swords with thick golden handles. A stink of gunpowder spread when *asafo* warriors fired their rifles into the air. Their fierce faces mismatched the smiles on the spectators who lined the road and shouted greetings to the honoured guests.

Enterprising locals set up tents along the road, selling beer and snacks to visiting mourners. Hawkers peddled souvenir T-shirts and baseball caps. Everyone wore red and black, except for the policemen in crisp white jackets and English "bobby" hats who directed traffic away from the parades. Men, fresh from the beer tents, were dazed and loud. Women sang. Children ran wild. On the shoreline, waves pounded a funeral march on the smooth boulders.

A special cloth was produced for the funeral. It was red and black, and featured an image of the dead chief along with words of condolence. The fabric, sewn into shirts and dresses, was worn by hundreds of men and women who were there to pay their respects. I tried to buy a *pagna* of the cloth, but the man at the shop told me they had been sold out for almost a month.

"A month? When did the chief die?"

"It has been nearly one year," he said.

"A year? Why haven't they buried him yet?"

"The chief was a great man. He was much loved by everybody. You see outside? All the music and dancers? All the tents and drummers? Dignitaries from everywhere are here to pay their respects. They say even the president is coming tomorrow. He will come in his helicopter. It takes time to prepare such a funeral. It is a very special day. You are very lucky to be in Ghana now. This does not happen very often."

"What did they do with his body for all this time?"

"They kept it in a refrigerator. On ice. Tomorrow they will bury him."

Outside, I followed the train of chiefs and mourners down the hill to Victoria Park. Only dignitaries were allowed into the arena but a security guard, on seeing my camera, waved me forward.

"You want to make picture? Come in."

"Are you sure it is okay?"

"Yes, yes. No problem. Welcome in Ghana."

The guard brought me past rows of mourners on plastic chairs, clapping their hands in the glow of a red plastic tarp. A man on a loudspeaker welcomed each dignitary into the arena:

> Now entering the square is Kofi Atta, honorable Chief of Dunkwa! We thank him for his generous gift of five crates of Star beer and eight crates of Fanta Orange! Welcome!

Meanwhile, a troupe of dancers waved red kerchiefs and stepped in the dust. An orchestra of sweaty drummers beat music out of drums adorned with breasts and phalluses. Young children eluded security, rushed into the arena and were scolded by stern elders. I took quick photos of all of this, feeling a bit intrusive, until my escort led me out of the arena. At the entrance a young Ghanaian in a boy scout uniform, his face covered with ritual scars, leaned against a statue of Queen Victoria.

I bought a strip of red cloth to tie around my cap and spent the rest of the day walking amid the crowds, swaying to music and ducking in and out of the beach-side beer tents. Countless locals greeted me and welcomed me to the funeral, to Cape Coast, to Africa. I met a local "prince" wearing a shirt and trousers made of shimmering gold cloth. I told him I liked his clothes and he offered to give me his shirt. Another man, an official of some kind, greet-

ed me and asked if I wanted to view the chief's body. He was surprised when I declined. I took my lunch at a food tent where a
banner read "Captain Joyce Welcomes You."

"You have come to see the funeral?" Joyce smiled as she filled
my bowl with yams and *palava*. "You are welcome. We are happy to
see visitors come and respect our culture and tradition. You are
welcome to Ghana."

Later, when she came to take away my empty bowl, she said,
"You like my *palava*? It is the best in Cape Coast. Next time you
come you must visit me and I will make you some more." I promised to return as feelings of acceptance washed away voyeuristic
unease.

But brief terror followed Joyce's hospitality. As I stepped outside the food tent an old woman charged at me from an alleyway
waving a machete over her head. I froze. Screaming, she swung the
blade in a wide arc in front of my neck, brought it down to the
ground and scraped a line in the road between us. Sparks jumped
from the blade and stung my sandalled feet, but I was too afraid to
move until she turned and walked away. Nearby a group of men
laughed so hard they spilled their food.

"She was going to cut off your head! You were so scared! Your
face turned many colours," one of them said.

"Why did she do that?" I asked, rubbing my throat.

"She is a crazy woman. She wanted to scare you."

"Do not worry. We would have buried you with the chief,"
another man said. "It would be a great honour." Their laughter rose
again and I, not knowing what else to do, laughed along with them.

I sat with the men for a few minutes and they told me of an
ancient Ghanaian burial tradition. Whenever a chief dies one of
his most trusted servants is killed and buried along with him. This
ensures the chief has reliable staff in the afterlife. This custom is
now illegal but there are still some villages—"in the north" the men
claimed—where dead chiefs are never buried alone.

"Maybe tomorrow the chief will take a white man with him,"
my friends joked before I left them and made my way up the road.

In front of Cape Coast Castle two men lurched towards me.

One said, "Brother! Please. Come here please." He wore a red head-band and a pair of sunglasses. His companion, eyes glazed with alcohol, had a live crab tied around his neck.

"Brother! Where are you from?" He reached out to shake my hand and almost lost his balance. "Please, you must talk to the crab."

"What?"

"You see the crab?" He pointed to his friend. "The crab is the totem animal of Cape Coast. You must talk to him," he raised his arms above his head with great drama and shouted to the sky, "out of respect for our departed chief!"

His friend let out a boozy chuckle and added, with great effort, "Crab."

"I don't know what to say to a crab."

"You can say anything you like. Talk about anything. Just give us one hundred *cedis* and you can talk to him."

"I have to pay to talk to the crab?"

"Yes. It is a great honour." His friend laughed again.

"No thank you," I said.

"No? Okay, but will you take our picture?"

I lifted my camera to my eye and said, "Smile." Both men grinned wide, but Crab Man's heavy eyes had trouble finding my lens. I snapped the photo, shook their hands and they walked away.

Before sundown I made my way to the taxi park and boarded a *tro-tro* for Biriwa, a small village a few kilometres west along the shoreline. I was going to stay at Anne's new home. A few weeks prior she moved her placement from Asawinso to the seaside. ("I'm from Victoria," she explained. "I need to hear the ocean.") On the *tro-tro* the man next to me introduced himself and offered me an avocado.

"How are you liking Ghana?" he asked.

"I love Ghana," I told him. I knew the claim sounded naïve, and that I was only a tourist after all, but I did love Ghana. How could I not love a place that treats strangers with such warmth, where drunk men wear live crabs and even death can be a song?

The next day Anne was busy marking her students' English

assignments. For their first assignment she had her students write a few lines about themselves and hand them in. One wrote

> I am twenty years of age. I am six feet tall with a nice round head. I have a smooth looking face. My complexion is admirably chocolate.

I took Ama, her host father's nine-year-old daughter, into Elmina for the afternoon. For a small fishing town, Elmina is a busy place. Children called out greetings as Ama and I walked past, and speeding taxis competed with the market goers for space on the narrow streets. I passed a small television shop called God Gives Electronics and laughed at a poster advertising a local band named Dan's Pee. All the roads in Elmina were lined with market stalls that sold everything from divine pineapples and palm oil, to plastic plates and soccer balls. Enthusiastic vendors waved auto parts at me, as if my backpack and I were in the market for a new carburetor.

The staple food in Elmina was smoked fish with *kenke*, a sour starchy mash made from fermented corn and wrapped in plantain leaves. The locals are very proud of their *kenke*. They insisted it was much better than what you find in Accra. I tried them both but couldn't make much of a judgment; with the ubiquitous red pepper sauce burning my mouth I could hardly taste the *kenke* at all.

To ease my blazing tongue I retreated into one of the numerous bars around town and ordered a Star beer for myself and a Fanta orange for Ama. Before long smiling locals joined us to talk about their relatives in Toronto, boast about the local *kenke* and ask me if I had come to visit "The Castle."

Perched on a rocky outcrop overlooking Elmina, The Castle has a sinister history dating back to its construction in 1482 by the Portuguese. The traders built St. George's Castle to protect their bustling West African gold trade. The Dutch seized the castle in 1637, established it as the African headquarters of the Dutch West Indies Trading Company, and expanded its storehouses to hold a commodity even more valuable than gold: slaves. Elmina Castle—

as it is now commonly called—became the first slave trading post in sub-Saharan Africa. The slave trade was so lucrative that the Dutch built another fort nearby, Fort St. Jago, to provide extra security.

Our visit to Elmina Castle was no lighthearted affair. Ama held my hand tight as our guide led us and a collection of mostly European and American visitors through the courtyards, ramparts, dungeons and officer's quarters housed within the castle's startlingly white walls. As a national monument and a UNESCO World Hernitage Site, Elmina Castle is extremely well maintained. Funding from overseas, much of it from the United States, goes into the upkeep of the structure. The walls literally shine in the Ghanaian sunlight, their whiteness a gleaming irony.

Our guide brought us through the spacious officer quarters and the courtyard where slave auctions were once held. Nowadays, this sunny space is used for musical performances and other cultural events. We climbed stairs to the bleached ramparts where silent cannons look out over the sea. Waves crashed against the stones at the base of the castle, reminders of the violence that occurred for centuries inside. From the ramparts we could see another castle only a few kilometres east. Because the Danes competed with the Dutch for control of the slave trade, they built this castle close enough to Elmina so that they could keep an eye on their rival's business but be out of cannon range.

The tour quickly headed out of the sun and into The Castle's dark interior. Our guide led us to the men's dungeon and warned us not to knock our foreheads on the low stone door frame on our way in. Only one person can pass through the door at a time, and I had trouble keeping hold of Ama. Once inside the smell of the room was shocking. The Portuguese kept gold in this room, but when the Dutch took over they turned it into a holding room for the slaves.

"Stevie Wonder came here," the guide said. "He touched the walls and he cried."

The floors beneath my pricey sandals were much higher than when they were originally built due to generations of accumulated blood, filth and excrement. Two hundred prisoners at a time were kept in these cramped and dark rooms, and sometimes, when the ships were late, for months. There was no room to lie down. The dungeon was damp and hot; outbreaks of yellow fever and malaria were commonplace. I could imagine the mosquitoes. Our guide pointed to the ceiling.

"Directly above this dungeon is the chapel where the Dutch went to pray."

We walked quietly to the women's dungeon, which was not as cramped as the men's. Female slaves were not as brutally treated as the men, but this was due to economics rather than mercy. Valued for their skills in cooking and housekeeping, female slaves fetched a higher price, so they were not as expendable as the men. Besides, the women were useful in other ways. Our guide gestured towards a stairwell in the back of the women's dungeon below a trap door in the ceiling.

"That door led to the governor's quarters. Each night he would come down the stairs and choose which of the women he would like to rape."

Even more sickening was the fact that these nightly assaults were a prisoner's only chance at salvation. A slave was set free if she became pregnant by an officer.

We walked the route the slaves took on their way to the ships and we passed a small holding area where the male slaves were branded. Often the men were so weakened by their treatment in the dungeons that the shock of the branding iron killed them instantly. As a final bit of torture male slaves were marched past the women's dungeon on their way to the ships. There the prisoners could see their spouses for the last time, but were forbidden to touch or cry out. The last holding area opened out to the sea through "The Door of No Return." After slaves passed through this portal they were led to the ships and were certain never to see their homeland again. During the height of the slave trade, over thirty thousand slaves passed through each year on their way to Brazil and the Caribbean. The Door has since been sealed with heavy bricks in a symbolic gesture that promises "Never Again." Each visitor touched the cold stones. Most everyone cried.

Suddenly ashamed of my white skin I looked down at Ama, surprised she was still holding my hand.

After the tour, Ama and I sat for a lunch of rice balls and groundnut soup. A man joined us and announced, "I love white people." Still shaking from my visit to the castle I asked him why.

"Because white man make car," he smiled.

This didn't make me feel any better.

I left Biriwa a few days later, promising to meet Anne in Togo when she finished her teaching term, and travelled along the coast in search of more castles. When I reached Fort Princes Town I turned into a ten-year-old boy.

Fort Princes Town, a secluded seaside village, was not on my map and could only be reached by taxi during the dry season; heavy rains turn the sandy road into a bog. There is a castle on a hill overlooking the village. It has seen many masters since it was built by the Prussians over three hundred years ago—Dutch merchants, African gold traders, British soldiers—but for a few days it belonged to me. I was alone there except for a silent watchman who patrolled the night with a kerosene lamp and a radio.

When I was young I dreamed of places like this and, with no one to see or scold me, I finally had my chance to play like a child. I spent my days climbing crumbling walls and finding hidden entrances that opened into the forest of weeds leading to the beach. I discovered storerooms and imagined them filled with gold, though all I saw was moss and lizards. I lost my breath leaping on ramparts and paused to catch it on silent, rusty cannons. Climbing the boulders to the seashore, I found secret swimming holes. For hours, I sat on stones and watched the waves and fishing boats. I jumped between rocks and over pockets of water and pretended my leaps were more dangerous than they really were.

Then the rain came, thick and loud, and I rushed back to lay siege to the castle. Ignoring the entrance I climbed the ramparts instead, jumping from ruin to ruin, being careful to avoid imaginary musket fire. The air stunk of gunpowder only I could smell. I was held captive in a dungeon and planned my escape through a door that hadn't been locked for a century. My trouser cuffs were wet with sea water, cold as they slapped across my bare ankles, and my shirt was filthy from climbing.

How long had it been since I felt this free? The joy and exercise made my chest hurt.

At night I wandered the hallways with a flashlight, tempting ghosts, but my nocturnal adventures made the watchman nervous. I returned to my room and slept on a mushy mattress, while sea breezes entered through the glassless windows.

I slept late in the mornings, drew water for my bath from a centuries-old well, and laid out wet clothes to dry on old stones. Once the caretaker collected my rent I walked down the hill in search of breakfast. Children played on the beach and collected stones to pitch at the goats who came to eat trash. At a primary school nearby uniformed students ran wild and spilled through classroom windows. I saw no teachers. When they spotted me the children waved, called out rhymes and begged for pens or coins:

> Bruni!
> *How are you?*
> *I am fine.*
> *Thank you.*
> *A pen?*

One afternoon, as I walked in the village, a familiar thumping sound signalled women were pounding *fufu* nearby. I followed the noise to a market stall. When it was ready they placed a ball of *fufu* in a bowl for me and smothered it with a soup made of fish and goat meat. I slurped my meal with the women and their brothers. The *fufu* was delicious but I was clumsy. Even after three months my fingers still hadn't learned to dine this way and my hosts laughed. Afterwards I joined the men for a warm Fanta—there were no refrigerators in Princes Town.

Before hiking back to the castle I stopped to buy bread, biscuits and a tin of sardines for my dinner. I passed a boy with a wheel-barrow full of coconuts. He chopped the hairy husk off a nut with a machete the size of his arm. Then he scalped it with a final stroke to create a hole to drink from. He handed it to me.

"The milk protects against malaria," he said.

After a couple of days alone in the castle, two other visitors arrived: an Australian who looked like Tarzan and his pretty Ghanaian girlfriend. He bought me a beer at the bar down the road, held his silent girlfriend's hand and asked me about my writing.

"Fort Princes Town is a very special place," he said. "I have been here before. It is very spiritual. The atmosphere will inspire you." I was thankful for the conversation, encouragement and warm beer, but was happy to see him go. I was ten years old, this was my castle and I didn't feel like sharing.

I left Fort Princes Town three days later. Only one car leaves for the coastal highway each day. It departed at sunrise and I had to get to the taxi park while it was still dark to make sure I got a seat. Just before we reached the highway our driver pulled the car over to the side of the road. The car was running fine and the road, while muddy from the night's rain, was passable. I couldn't understand why we stopped.

The driver pulled an empty jerry can out from under his seat and filled it with water at a well next to the road. When he returned, he took a rag from the back seat, poured the water on the roof and began washing the taxi. It took about fifteen minutes, and four trips back to the well to refill the jerry can, before the taxi was deemed clean enough to drive. All the while the passengers waited patiently and without complaint. The driver returned to his seat, replaced the jerry can and continued the journey. Nobody said a word.

My taxi dropped me in Takoradi. There I found transport up the central highway, via Kumasi, to visit the town of Tamale in northern Ghana, and watched as the tropics of the coast faded into the dust of the hotter, drier north. This was a different Ghana. In the north, houses made of red mud grow from the soil like appendages of the earth. They are no less organic than the mango trees that painted shadows across dirt roads. The red soil owned that world. It stained the white walls of the Barclay's Bank, the hems of long dresses and the pages of my journal. On hot afternoons trucks rattled down the main road and sprayed water to keep the dust down. But the sun was quick, the dust stubborn, and Tamale grew back into copper from the ankles up.

It was calmer in Tamale than in Accra or Cape Coast. Everything moved slower, as if impeded by the dust and heat. Streets were quiet—there were far more bicycles than trucks—and the market, even at the height of the day's commerce, was free of frenzy and noise.

"Why is northern Ghana so much quieter than the south?" I asked the woman who sold boiled yams at the market.

"It is because we are Muslim."

Christianity is noisy in southern Ghana. Street preachers weave through the markets and motor parks shouting gospel verses at the sky. The faithful christen their children with names like Wonder and Blessing, and radio stations play equal parts highlife and gospel music. There were more denominations than I could keep track of, and I wondered how a faith so convoluted could be so loud. But in Tamale, where domes rather than steeples ruled the skyline, religion was quiet, unassuming and respectful. Like Denu's three silent Muslims.

I was reminded of Jennifer, another Crossroads volunteer, who told me she was a better Christian in Ghana. She prayed and attended church for the first time in years. Other volunteers told me the same. Did they suddenly believe again? Was it the strange environment and distance from home that urged them towards spiritual comfort, or was this a case of mob piety? I wonder what happened to their new religious fervour and renewed faith when they returned home?

I spent an afternoon on a bicycle and pedalled slowly along the dusty streets. I followed a herd of cattle to auction. There, I watched a butcher at work. He stood over a cow carcass and hacked away at its flesh with a machete. Blood and bits of bone flew everywhere. Meanwhile, a pickup truck full of dead sheep arrived and a crowd of men heaved the bloodied corpses onto the ground. I rode away, mildly sickened but strangely euphoric, finding a sort of honesty in the unapologetic gore.

One night the National Cultural Centre in Tamale screened the Antonio Banderas film *Desperado*. I'm not sure how a movie starring Banderas and a crew of Latino gunmen qualified as Ghanaian culture but I bought my ticket nonetheless. As a prelude to the film, several old Tina Turner and Michael Jackson music videos were shown. Then came Antonio, guns blazing.

The Ghanaian crowd at the Centre loved the film, although the scenes that lacked violence and sex were largely ignored. Luckily there were very few of these. According to a poster outside, the next movie at the Centre would be a lesbian porn film. I wondered what the assistant headmaster at Three Town would think.

After the film I walked to Club Enesta, a bar where the music was thick and the beer startlingly cheap. I sat next to a meaty Ghanaian man with a glass of Star in his hand. He looked at me and his smile became the brightest thing in the dim room. Jonathan was a soldier with the Ghanaian army and spent much of his military career as a United Nations peacekeeper. He saw action in nearly all of the world's trouble spots in the last decade.

"The world is a hot, hot place," he said.

I wanted to hear more about this, about the world from an African soldier's eyes, but Jonathan preferred to talk about the foreign women he bedded while on assignment.

"There was a French girl and a Dutch woman. I love the Dutch. And in Cyprus an Italian woman. Her name was Cecilia. She was the best, my friend. The Italian women are something. Have you been with an Italian woman before?"

I gulped down my beer and added my own sexual exploits to the conversation. I exaggerated when I didn't outright lie and invented an international crew of former lovers. There is a freedom that anonymity makes possible and beer-borne bravado fuels. This was a favourite game, becoming somebody else for a few minutes. I relished the pleasant sort of sleaziness until, as if on cue, I heard female voices ascending the stairwell. Jonathan and I turned to see a dozen white European women enter the bar. Most were in their early twenties and smartly dressed in tight shirts and long, elegant skirts. They wore lipstick and perfume. In the reddish grime of the Enesta, a bar that until this moment was an all-male preserve of boasting soldiers and spilled beer, these girls seemed a hallucination. They paused in the doorway, let their eyes adjust to the gloom, then retreated to a table in the back.

I gave them the polite wave foreigners seem obligated to exchange and they invited me to join them. Jonathan was immediately jealous; he assumed I was headed for romance.

"I like the blonde one," he said as I stood up from my stool.

They were a group of young development students from Germany. They were on a six-week exchange to determine how to best help Ghana. They were enthusiastic, well-meaning and excited to share with me their solutions for Ghana's "problems."

"What Ghana needs," one said, "is for every family to have a car. That way the women would not have to walk to the well to fetch water. They could just drive there instead and it would save them so much time."

Another added, "That is very true, but I think it is more important for Ghanaians to have better access to the Internet. We found out that very few Ghanaians have computers. Did you know this? With the Internet they could see how other people live and learn how to live better."

"But most Ghanaian villages don't have electricity," I countered.

"Yes they do," she said.

Jonathan's favourite blonde disagreed. "I think the major problem for Ghana is they think too much about slavery."

"What do you mean?" I asked.

"Have you been to Elmina and Cape Coast? Have you seen the slave castles?"

"Yes."

"Don't you think the Ghanaians are too fixated on what happened to them in the past? All they talk about is slavery. Slavery was bad, but it ended hundreds of years ago. Ghanaians need to get over it, forget about it, and get on with their lives. They need to think about the future and not worry about the past."

"You think they should forget about slavery?" Most of the table started to nod. I couldn't believe it. My beery nerve spoke for me. "I think you're all crazy."

The table erupted and suddenly, against my better judgement, I was arguing poverty and economics with a fevered group of what I thought were naïve Germans. They scoffed when I said computers and cars are not what Africa needs. When I suggested that Africa doesn't need saving from the West and that Africa has lessons to teach the rest of the world, the Germans laughed at me. They thought *I* was naïve. I had no ammunition against such confident ignorance, and I felt my blood getting hot.

Finally, to illustrate her point, one of the students turned to a Ghanaian man sitting at the table beside us.

"Excuse me sir, but we are having a debate. Can you tell me what is it you need more than anything else?"

"A car. Like you," he said, and broke my heart.

A few days later I met Cesar on the *tro-tro* from Tamale to Nakpanduri. He was a recent convert to Christianity. Cesar used to be a Muslim "but Muslims believe too much in *juju*, which is the work of Satan," he said. "So now I live for Jesus Christ. Are you a Christian?" I told him I was raised Catholic and this spared me a sermon.

Cesar's conversion came after the mysterious death of his father, a village elder.

"One day my father, who was a big man in the village, was addressing a group of elders. Some of my father's political rivals were there. He was speaking and suddenly he lost his voice. He tried three times to speak and then he fell from the podium. He was dead."

"What happened to him?" I asked.

"He was shot by a slingshot. An invisible, spiritual slingshot. One of his rivals had strong *juju* and they killed him. I saw with my own eyes."

"You saw the slingshot?"

"No. I said the slingshot is invisible. I saw my father fall and die."

Cesar gave me an orange. In Ghana, street vendors scrape the zest off green oranges and sell the naked fruit for a couple coins each. To eat them you bite a hole in the top of the orange and squeeze the juice into your mouth and spit out the seeds. When the orange is dry the remains get tossed out the *tro-tro* window. Everywhere in Ghana the ground is littered with the corpses of sucked out oranges.

Cesar and I sat quietly until our *tro-tro* passed Gambaga. He said, "Will you visit Gambaga?" I told him I hadn't planned it. "It is unfortunate," he said. "There are plenty of things to see there."

Apparently Gambaga boasts two strange attractions. The first is the famous "Witches Village." Cesar told me that when a man or woman is convicted of using black magic they are given a special potion and then exiled to a poor neighbourhood on the outskirts of Gambaga.

"They must live in the Witches' Village forever. That is their punishment."

"What is the potion for?"

"The potion takes away their magic. When they drink it they can never use *juju* to harm anybody again. Still, even after they take the potion, they can see spiritually."

"Can they see invisible slingshots?"

"Yes," he nodded. "That is right."

The other attraction stems from a legend about one of Gambaga's former paramount chiefs. When a chief dies his son is responsible for paying tribute to his deceased father, but this particular chief had no sons. The villagers had to make alternate arrangements for his funeral. They decided to build a wall in his honour. Since the man was well-respected they used milk and honey for mortar and human bodies for bricks. I asked Thomas if the wall was still standing.

"No. Most of the wall has fallen down. It is difficult to find the ruins, but if you look closely you can see parts of it still."

"What did it look like?"

"It looks just like a regular wall. Seven years ago, my school went on an excursion to Gambaga. We came to see the Witches Village and the wall. It was very interesting. A good excursion."

I told him that on my school field trips we usually went to the zoo. He found this fascinating.

Cesar was let out in Nalerigu. An eight-year-old girl took his place on the seat next to me. Her face was marked with ritual scars.

Facial scarification is common in Ghana; I stopped noticing the rough slashes that decorated so many cheeks and temples. Even the headmaster at Three Town had a small horizontal cut under his eye. He didn't like to talk about it. "It is a ritual from when I was a boy," he said when I asked. Then he quickly changed the subject. But the girl next to me on the *tro-tro* was different: her entire face was scarred. An intricate pattern of incisions formed a web over her cheeks, and tiny symbols were etched into the flesh next to her eyes. The designs were precise and clean, and reminded me of lace. In the sunlight the fine lines gleamed silver, like spider silk, and nearly disappeared each time the truck passed through shade.

I know I was supposed to find this scarification barbaric. When I saw this girl's face I was supposed to see pain. I was supposed to imagine rivulets of tears running into blood, and a rusty blade carving her flesh. I was supposed to feel repulsed.

I was not supposed to see beauty.

When I reached Nakpanduri the guest house was under renovation and officially closed. The owner wasn't around but the work crew was happy to take my money and let me stay. The guest house was on the edge of the Gambaga Escarpment. From there the view stretched into Burkina Faso. I spent my days sitting on the edge of the cliffs, listening to birds and swinging my feet over the edge, feeling daring and childlike. I heard that elephants wandered the valley floor but the forest was too thick to spot them from the cliff. I hiked down into the valley and stood guard near a watering hole in case the elephants emerged. They never did. Instead I watched a trio of village women pile firewood on their heads and hike up the steep road back to Nakpanduri. I followed them back to the village, marvelling at their stamina and balance. They walked steady and quick under their heavy loads while I, unencumbered, paused regularly to catch my breath and wipe the sweat from my eyes. After my hike I found thin refreshment in two bottles of warm orange Fanta. There were only two refrigerators in Nakpanduri, both ran on kerosene and were broken.

That night the carpenters at the guest house invited me to join them for dinner. There were three workmen and a woman whose duties, from what I could gather, were to prepare their meals, wash their clothes and have sex with the foreman. We discussed sexual politics in Ghana, a topic we discussed over *fufu*, okra stew and guinea fowl soup.

"Women in Ghana," the foreman said, "will sleep with many, many men. And when they get pregnant they will go to the man with the most money and say, 'This is your baby.' If she cannot convince him, she will go to the next richest man and say again, 'This is your baby.' She will keep doing this until she convinces a man to be responsible for the child, but she will look for the richest man first."

I looked to the woman to see her reaction to this claim. She nodded. "It is true. Women are more wicked than men. They are much more wicked." Everyone agreed.

One of the other men offered a solution. "When I have sex with a women, I always wear a condom. And when I finish I take it off and show it to her like this." He mimed swinging a used condom in a woman's face. "Then I say, 'You see? If you get pregnant it is not from me.'" We all laughed at this.

One of the men turned to me and asked, suddenly serious, "Is it true that AIDS was invented by Americans to kill black people?"

"No, of course not. Why would you think that?"

"Many people believe this."

"Do you?"

"I don't know," he said and changed the subject. "Is it true that people from another planet landed in the United States?"

"I'm not sure. Many people believe it's true."

"I believe it," he said. "And I heard about Atlantis. Do you know it? There was a country called Atlantis. It was an island and one day there was a great earthquake and the whole country sunk under the ocean. All the people learned to breathe under water and they live there still. Nobody knows where it is."

"I don't believe that."

"Why not?"

"If I brought you to the river right now and pushed you under the water, would you learn to breathe?"

He thought for a moment and laughed. "You are right. You are right. I would drown."

I travelled from Nakpanduri to Bunkpurudu, a small village on the border with Togo. Leaving Nakpanduri was no small feat. Vehicles passing through the town were scarce, and I waited beside the road for seven hours before a white pickup truck pulled up. The priest who was driving it was reluctant to give me a ride, but the officials at the police stop demanded it. So I enjoyed a rare free ride—born of police coercion—in the back of a truck along with some sacks of rice, a rusty bicycle and three ill-fated chickens.

Bunkpurudu was as close to the middle of nowhere as I had been. Every building was made of mud and thatch, even the guest house. As far as I could tell Bunkpurudu was a farming community. Stalks of corn and millet grew tall, giving the place something of a claustrophobic feel. Upon my arrival I met Alan, the local customs boss and the self-professed "Big Man" in the village. He treated me to beers at the guest house and introduced me to his mother and Munira, his sister.

Munira had a reputation in Bunkpurudu for being a marvellous cook. She invited me into her home for dinner that evening—goat stew and boiled yams—which she fed me with quiet pride. She talked to me as I ate, and laughed when I burned my fingers on the hot yams.

"White men have hands that are too sensitive. You must wait until the yams cool a little."

Munira's youngest son, a three year old named Ahmed, quickly adopted me as his new best friend, but he had trouble pronouncing my name and giggled at every attempt. Munira has another son who lives with her ex-husband in Saskatoon, of all places. His name is Vincent and she showed me a picture of him. He is an "albino" boy, with light skin and hair that looked like spun copper.

"You must write a letter to Vincent when you return to Canada. Tell him his mother is well, but misses him very much." She said this softly, like a prayer.

Munira was beautiful, simply but breathtakingly so. I sat with her after dark on her porch as the rains came down, looking out into a darkness broken only by lightning. In the distance I heard the sound of radios, but next to me Munira was singing to her son as he squirmed on and over and under her knees. The rain and darkness heightened the scents of everything. I could smell the wet millet stalks across the road, the pots of stew and yam peelings, a tin of kerosene. Munira's soft songs, the darkness of that night and the sound and smells that only rain can bring washed over me and filled me with peace.

The serenity of that night became greater considering the violence of the following afternoon. I bid Munira my thanks and farewell, shook little Ahmed's hand and walked the three kilometres to the customs house on the border with Togo. The customs post was a small cement structure with a desk, a file cabinet, a small prison cell and, oddly enough, a boy with wild eyes tied to a tree outside. As villagers passed by on their way to and from Togo they were obliged to dismount from their vehicles and surrender their baggage to be checked by the officials, one of whom was Alan. This customs check was only a formality and one that didn't appear to be rigorously enforced. Rarely were bags checked, and as long as people slowed down at the gate, they were allowed to pass through without being stopped.

I hoped to cross the border into Togo from Bunkpurudu but it turned out the customs post did not have any immigration authority. I could not get my passport stamped and so my entry into Togo would have been illegal. This meant that when I tried to leave Togo later in the month I would be at the mercy of the Togolese officials, and would likely have to pay a generous bribe. So I decided to return to Bunkpurudu for the night and take the midnight bus to Bawku where I could cross into Togo legally. Alan promised he would use his great influence in Bunkpurudu to ensure I had a seat on the bus.

I asked Alan about the boy tied to the tree.

"This is a foolish boy. We caught him carrying wee smoke into Togo. He comes down the road very fast, and he did not stop at the gate. If he stopped we would have let him through without checking him, but he is foolish. We catch him and we find this in his pocket." Alan showed me a small bag of marijuana. "So we will leave him there for some time to teach him a lesson. Maybe we will beat him. But for now we will keep him tied up."

Alan paused and looked up into the fierce midday sun. He untied the boy from the tree and bound him instead to the gate that blocked the road. Now the boy was exposed to the direct heat of a Ghanaian afternoon. A much more suitable torture.

"It is very hot today. Ha! Ha! He will learn a good hot lesson." Apparently the heat was getting to Alan too, and he asked me if I wanted some cold beer. I did, and he sent one of his officers, Kofi, across the border to fetch a few bottles.

"You will have to wait," Alan said, "the nearest town is some distance away."

When I asked him why he didn't send the officer back into Bunkpurudu for beers Alan replied, "Togolese beer is much better than the beer in Ghana."

We sat waiting for refreshment in the shade of the customs post. Alan pulled out the package of marijuana again and turned it over in his hands.

"What are you going to do with it?" I asked.

Alan didn't know. "I will probably throw it away. Throw it in a fire." He paused and looked at me.

"Have you smoked wee before?"

"Not in Ghana, but in Canada I smoke sometimes."

"Does it make you a fool?"

"What do you think? Do I seem like a fool to you?" He laughed. I was going to offer to roll him a joint but decided against it.

Alan and I talked about Canada, and he asked to see my camera.

"If you were going home today I would ask you to give this to me," he insisted. "Cameras are easy to buy in Canada, and money is easy to earn."

I tried to convince Alan that the West isn't quite the utopia of opportunity and endless wealth he imagined, but he wouldn't believe me. Instead of arguing I looked outside to the sweating prisoner.

He was gone. Only the bit of rope that had bound his hands remained, laying mockingly in the dust beneath the gate.

"Alan, the boy has escaped."

Alan jumped up and ran outside looking up and down the road. There was no sign of the prisoner. He started to curse. I couldn't believe the boy had the courage to escape. I was proud of him, a little, and I tried hard to suppress my smile. Alan's anger soon faded, and he shook his head and laughed.

"That foolish boy! His brain is funny with wee smoke. I cannot believe he ran away. I should have used my handcuffs on the little devil!"

"Why didn't you?"

"They are locked in the cabinet and I lost the key."

Our fugitive's escape was short-lived. The poor devil ran right into Kofi as he returned from fetching beer. A few minutes later we saw them coming up the road. A large man in uniform, with six cold Togolese beers in one hand and a crying boy in the other. Judging by their expressions it was clear that both knew the kind of terror one was about to inflict on the other. Our boy had taken a big gamble trying to escape.

Alan and another officer tied the boy to the gate once again and returned to the shade of the customs post. Beers were opened and Alan, myself and the other officers enjoyed the cool, strong Togolese brew. Between swigs the officers took turns beating the boy with their batons, while I sat and watched. It was surreal, sipping beer to the sound of slaps, punches and screams. The loud crack of wood on skull. But I was the only one who was disturbed by this. It was a game to everyone else, and the men argued about whose turn it was to lay their boots on the recaptured fugitive. (Kofi, the captor, went first.) I half-expected Alan to ask if I would like a turn beating the boy, but he never did.

The beer was finished quickly, and the officers now focused their full attention on torturing their captive. They brought him inside, into the small prison cell, and told him they were going to bring him to the prison in Tamale. At this he doubled his screams. I couldn't imagine the horrors of a Ghanaian prison, but this boy could. He spent twenty minutes in the cell with two beer-inspired soldiers, and even through the thick cement walls, I could hear his cries, their barked threats and the repeated whack of batons.

When I wrote about this in my journal Alan asked what I was writing. I told him I was writing about how good the beer is in Africa. He liked that.

Togo

"I have a pistol."

I look up into wild red eyes and a face darkened by stubble and scars. I don't know what is happening until I see his knife. Not a pistol, thank god. I turn to James and see him lift Anne's camera from her bag, and suddenly I understand.

Then he is on the sand with us. There is a knife in my face. Someone pushes a hand in my pocket and my wallet is gone. The knife man flips through my cards and bills. His movements are nervous and twitchy and I realize I am calmer than he is. James empties Anne's bag on the sand.

The knife is short and rusty with a red leather handle like the knives in the souvenir markets—a tourist knife. How fitting. I stare at the blade and wonder if I can move fast enough. He reads my mind, bares his teeth and the blade flies and bites.

I don't feel it cut me. I don't feel afraid. I don't feel anything and this surprises me.

He moves towards Anne.

"Wait," he says. "Wait." He grabs her, his rough hands on her thighs, her breasts, and red terror washes over me. My fists turn to stone and violence *bubbles in my muscles like lava. But he stops before I erupt; he only wants her hidden wallet. She cries and begs for her passport. Then it is over.*

I don't know why I chase them. There is no logic to this tardy heroism. I hear my boots splash in the surf. They are heavy with sea water and I am wet to my knees. James is fast and far ahead, but I catch up to the knife man. He hears me coming and turns and charges.

"I will kill you!" he spits as the knife flies in front of my chest. "You are crazy? I will kill you!" and the knife comes again. Over the sound of waves I hear the blade split the air in front of my throat. I freeze. He turns and runs, and this time I don't chase him.

How far have I run? What time is it? I am tired and my lungs hurt. My legs burn under wet trousers. I can't see anything. I walk until I hear my name, and then I am holding someone sobbing, kissing trembling arms.

In our hotel room I see the cut on my hand. It isn't much more than a scratch but I don't show Anne. I don't want her to worry.

On our first day in Togo, Anne and I were robbed. I'd met Anne that morning in Lomé at Hotel Mawu Li. She'd finished her volunteer placement a few days earlier and endured a tearful farewell to her friends in Biriwa. We spent the afternoon visiting the colourful Lomé marketplace and eating avocado sandwiches from the streetside food vendors. We met our guide James on the beach. He was friendly and welcoming. He gave us some free postcards and we, foolish and cheap, sold him our trust.

After the robbery we returned to our hotel, where, fortunately, we'd left most of our money. We sat on the bed and looked at the postcards James gave us when we first met him. I wrote the story of the robbery on the back of mine and address it to a friend back home. Anne tore hers to pieces and burned them with her cigarette lighter. We had very little in common.

The next morning two men on a motorcycle drove by our hotel, tossed a package into the front door and sped away. It was Anne's bag. Inside was her passport, our driver's licenses, my Social Insurance card and student ID. These items were useless to our thieves, but instead of throwing them away they returned them to us. I couldn't understand this generosity, and I was uncomfortable feeling gratitude towards men who betrayed, robbed and cut me. Even my rage had been stolen. I couldn't decide if this was a good thing.

We wanted to get out of Lomé so Anne and I hired a canoe in Agbodrafo to take us to Togoville, which is across Lac Togo from the coastal highway, a stretch of dusty road that spans this sliver of a nation in less than ninety kilometres. We were weary from arguing with each other all day and stayed quiet the entire trip, responding to our captain's friendly questions with inappropriately curt, one word answers. It was not a good day. Further, hotel rooms in Togoville were expensive and Anne and I found ourselves sharing a single bed in a tiny room. I dreaded the night's snores and blanket politics.

I hardly remember what we were arguing about. I grew impatient with her slowness at the textile shops, and she grew angry at my impatience. Something like that. Childish things. Our friendship, it seemed, died on that beach in Lomé

Anne and I decided to return to Ghana because we both felt safe there. She met some Canadian software salesmen at the embassy and they let us take refuge in their rented house. We used their phone to cancel stolen credit cards and order replacement traveller's cheques—and to call our mothers—but mostly we wanted out of Africa for a little while. This modern house in a distant Accra suburb, complete with satellite television, air conditioning and hot shower, was as close to home as we could find. I wanted to stay until my enthusiasm for travel returned, or at least until I stopped feeling the phantom blade in my palm.

For days after the robbery I felt the pain of the thief's knife cutting my hand, though the scratch itself dissolved. My flesh remembered each tiny imperfection in the blade, each speck of rust. The sensation kept me awake at night, fuelled nightmares. During the day I rubbed my hands together constantly, hoping to erase the scar I couldn't see but couldn't stop feeling.

Those days trapped with Anne were misery. She blamed me for

the robbery, and perhaps she had reason. I trusted James. I befriended him in town that afternoon, invited him out with us that night and let him guide us to the beach. Anne said her instincts warned her about him, that she never really trusted his intentions. I wondered why she never mentioned these suspicions until afterwards, but I didn't ask. We didn't talk much in Accra. Instead we walked silently around the big house, avoiding each other's eyes, burning our time with movies on television and out-dated Canadian magazines, hoping that these little bits of home could distract us from the fact that we didn't like Africa, or each other, very much anymore.

After four days we decided to return to Togo. "We have to con-front our fears," Anne said. Neither of us mentioned the tension in the house was making it hard to breathe. Travelling together, though, was only slightly better than staying still. Our tempers were raw, every Togolese man seemed a thief and every glance from Anne reminded me that it was all my fault. I'd ruined everything.

"I'm going to find something to eat," I said after claiming a cor-ner of our new room in Togo for my pack. "You coming?"

She pulled a long drag off her cigarette, lifted her chin and blew smoke at the ceiling. We shared accommodation before and she knew I hated when she smoked in the room. "No," she said before taking another drag. I left the hotel.

It was late in the afternoon and the marketplace was nearly empty. There was an old woman sitting under the loose thatch of a market stall, selling rice and beans from a blue pail. I approached her and she grinned at me, her smile a scattering of orange teeth and her face a blossom of deep wrinkles. I touched my fingertips to my lips. She nodded slowly and patted the bench next to her, inviting me to sit close. She lifted a clean bowl and spoon from a wash basin then looked at me. Tilted her head. Waited for me to answer. I held out a 100 *franc* coin. She nodded again and filled my bowl with food, tapping her spoon against the plastic rim to free sticky, fugitive rice. She added sauce and paused between each spoonful to watch for my nod that told her "enough." I ate in silence. She watched, flattered by my appetite, and waited for me to finish. Then she took the bowl away and filled it again. A gift for a stranger. I finished just as the fading sun turned dusty ground to copper. I handed her my coin and walked away.

There are poems that have no words. I read them in the moments of ordinary days, by the light of solitude and quiet. I almost forgot this is the only way to see them. I returned to the hotel room and told Anne that in the morning, after breakfast, I would be travelling alone.

"Seek out the fruits of silence and gather them up."

These words were written in my room at the Abbaye de l'Acsension monastery in the hills of western Togo. I'd arrived there early in the day, a few days after leaving Anne in Togoville. There I sat quiet in the forest that surrounded the monastery and found some peace in a country that greeted me with violence.

I'd forgotten what the words "silence" and "privacy" meant. I'd rarely been alone since I'd arrived in Africa. Quiet times reading books or sitting on the beach in Denu were always shortened by curious locals looking to befriend the white man. Hushed forest walks were marred by the presence of requisite guides and the children who always followed, giggling and begging. Only in sleep did I find silence, and that, too, was short-lived, ended early by village noises, barking dogs and morning heat.

But it was peaceful at the Abbaye. In the morning, white mist embraced the monastery and gave shelter from the noisy outside. As the whiteness drifted past, colours become less distinct. Everything felt connected by the pervading and visible ether. There is great peace in such a palpable connectedness. This was my favourite time of the day, before the sun of late morning burned away the misty veil and brought the surrounding green into sharp focus. Although the monastery housed a faith I'd abandoned I could not help but feel as if I was on sacred ground. The silence urged me to pause, and I was in no hurry to leave.

For three days I embraced the schedule, if not the conviction, of a Benedictine monk. I rose with the church bells each day at five o'clock, six on Sunday, made my way to the chapel for morning prayers, then went back to my room for an ice cold shower. The day continued with four more services in the chapel interspersed with quiet meals and slow walks. My day ended where it began, in the chapel listening to the faithful lift their voices heavenward.

The chapel was a simple structure that smelled of wet wood and lingering incense. In the early mornings the white mists entered through the large windows and settled on the pews like early believers. The floor was stone and the vaulted ceiling curved into a dome with a portal that opened to sunlight and sky. Altars, pulpits and candlesticks were sculpted from wood and depicted lions, palm trees and drums. A carving of a black man knocking a cocoa pod from a tree supported one altar. There was no pipe organ, only a collection of rattles, wooden xylophones called *balafons,* and *djembe* drums. The Jesus hanging from the lone crucifix was a black man. White missionaries may have brought Catholicism to Togo, but this was not a white man's church. There were no frescoes of a blanched white Jesus, no pale Virgins. This was the first church I'd seen in Africa that suggested Christianity was adopted by these people, not shackled to them.

It was the music that brought me to the chapel for each service, especially the melodies that flowed from the kora. A kora is a twenty-one string African lute made of rosewood, cowhide and gourd. The sound was strange and haunting, and filled the church like liquid. The kora stood upright on the floor on a wooden stand. A thin monk sat on a stool in front of it and played with both hands. His fingers graced the strings, the music slipping in and out of minor chords. These were not the hymns I knew. They sounded like love songs.

The kora player accompanied a chorus of singing *frères.* I didn't know enough French to understand their hymns so the sound was pure art to me, simplified and unburdened by meaning. Their voices poured directly into me, unfiltered by my intellect, and filled me with great calm.

Meals were another joy. The dining hall was separated into two large rooms, one reserved for the monks and the other for visitors like myself. Meals were eaten in silence. The only sound save for the click of fork on plate was the broadcasted voice of a monk reading scripture.

During my first meal at the monastery a small plate of fried fish and potatoes appeared alongside large bowls of delicious Togolese *pâte,* a grey, spongy strach, and okra stew. Nobody touched this fish; I, along with my African companions opted for tasty African fare. This was the best African food I had ever tasted, and I ate a bellyful. After our plates were cleared a woman who sat next to me asked me why I did not eat the plate of fish that the chef had prepared especially for me. Apparently there was some concern that I, the white stranger, would not enjoy traditional African food, so the "European-style" fish and chips was for me.

After we finished the meal we took a cue from one of the monks and rose in unison to bow our heads again in prayer. Then everyone marched into the kitchen and washed the dishes together. Again not a word was spoken while we focused completely on this mundane task. In the absence of talk, washing plates and glasses became a meditation, the clinking of silverware against metal bowls a hymn. It is strange how holy everything seems when not soiled by speech.

My deepest religious experience occurred during breakfast one morning. Real coffee—rich and dark—appeared like an angel. It had been months since I had a real cup of coffee. My caffeine addiction was serviced by bitter Nescafé which tasted more like chemicals than coffee. The monks grew coffee beans, as well as cocoa and peppermint, in the nearby hills. I drank so much holy brew I trembled like a Shaker for the rest of the day. Later I bought two pounds from the small shop operated by the monks to raise funds for the monestary.

The monks also sold postcards depicting African versions of biblical scenes. The Last Supper shows an African Jesus and his twelve apostles drinking wine from a calabash. Bethlehem is a village of mud huts with thatched roofs. I bought some of the cards, sent one to my grandmother and wondered what she would think of it. I also bought a wooden crucifix medallion but I never wore it.

I stayed for five days at the Abbaye and must have been something of an enigma for the monks. I didn't speak enough French to understand or participate in any of the church services, yet I attended all five each day. I was a white man with shaggy hair wearing African clothes, who had a huge appetite for African food and ignored the European dishes prepared especially for me. I didn't wear my crucifix, instead a twisted copper bracelet worn by fetish priests circled my wrist. I must have baffled the poor monks.

I travelled from the monastery to Aného. While I wandered the streets of Aného one night, I heard drumming and followed the sound down an alleyway. A group of boys huddled in front of a private home were peering through a crack in the gate. There was a party inside. Thirty villagers sat in a circle near a table crowded with bottles of beer and spirits. Men played *djembe* drums and cowry-shell rattles. Women in bright cloth danced and sang, their voices filling the dusk like smoke. I joined the boys at their peephole until a man emerged from inside. The boys scattered but the man, seeing me, stepped aside and opened the gate wide.

"*Wazo*," he said.

Inside every face turned and welcomed me with smiles. Two men shifted on a bench to make room for me and someone handed me a glass of pastis.

I sat for a half-hour with my hosts and watched as they drummed and danced and sang. They took turns dancing in the centre, eyes closed, heads tilted upwards and faces split with grins. Some shook fly wisps made of horse hair as they stepped and spun in the sand. They urged me to dance and I, emboldened by their liquor and hospitality, tried to mimic the chicken-like dance. My missteps earned applause and more pastis. After the dancing two women performed a short play. They spoke in Ewe and I couldn't understand a word, but the others laughed at every mysterious joke. I turned and saw that the young voyeurs had returned to their crack in the gate. Strangely embarrassed, I gave them a wave.

During the play a man whispered in my ear. "Where from?" he

asked. I told him Canada and he asked, "Canada is good?"

I wanted to tell him that in Canada my family does not celebrate this way. There are no drums or dancing, and too often drinking stands in for joy. I wanted to say that I'd never felt as welcome
and respected as I did there, a million miles from home, and that
Canada treats strangers with suspicion and fear more often than
kindness. I wanted to admit that in Canada, if I saw someone
eavesdropping on my family, I'd probably chase him away myself.

Instead I said, "Yes. Canada is good."

As I continued to move through Togo, I felt an energy fill my lungs
like wind. It was unsettling, and when it passed through my body I
felt it take away certainty and science. My "civilized" frown melted
in the heat; I became unexpectedly pliable and soft. My armour fell
away, plate by plate, and while sometimes this scared me, most
often I found it beautiful. In Africa my skepticism was inappropriate, a raincoat in the desert. Most incredible of all is that I caught
myself believing.

I visited Glidji for the annual *Yeké-Yeké* festival of the Guin people. The weekend-long celebration honours the elders and rings in
a new year for the Guin. *Yeké-Yeké*'s main event is the unveiling of a
sacred stone, the colour of which would divine the fortunes of the
Guin in the coming year. The stone's unveiling follows an elaborate
ritual that takes place in a dusty outdoor auditorium. I paid for a
seat in the main arena to witness the event.

Twenty women filed into the arena. Some wore silver starfish
and butterflies in their hair. Others wrapped their heads in gleaming white turbans. Wrists, ankles and earlobes hung heavy with
metal charms. Many women were naked to the waist and had white
paint streaked down their arms and breasts. Strings of cowry shells
and fat beads hung from their necks. Their silver adornments
reflected the light of the afternoon in sudden flashes of white, and
the women sparkled like stars. But the sunshine that played off
their jewellery belied their serious faces.

Drummers began to play in the wings of the arena and the women started swaying to the music. The dance was slow and deliberate at first, as if their limbs were weighed down by silver. With seeming effort they raised their arms to the sky and lowered their palms to the ground to thank the gods for a generous harvest. But as the drums' tempo increased, so did the dance. The women stepped swiftly in the dust, their hops matching the drummers' quickened rhythms. Their movements became wilder, as if the music gradually lightened their limbs. The faster they moved, the more they gleamed, and their rattling jewellery added to the musical arrangement. Still, even as their bodies became more overwhelmed with dance, their faces remained severe.

One dancer fell out of step with the others. She walked forward out of the dancing line and fell to her knees. She bent forward, placed her forehead in the dust and started to shake. The other women looked down at her but kept dancing. I felt the crowd around me hold their breath, then whisper to each other. I was the only one who didn't know what was happening.

When the woman lifted her face to the crowd her eyes were rolled back in her head. Clumsily she stood up, flung her arms in the air and screamed at the sky. When she collapsed again one of the other dancers came to her aid, lifted her up and led her away from the arena, passing me on the way out. The woman was sweating, breathing fast and growling.

One by one each of the dancers fell into trance until the arena was filled with seizures and mania. The crowd watched, uncomfortably, as women surrendered their bodies to whatever forces borrowed them. They threw themselves into the audience, collapsed in shaking heaps and howled at the sunshine. Their eyes shut tight and sprung open again. Sometimes I saw glazed blankness in their eyes; other times, unknown terror. One woman threw herself at a soldier's legs, embarrassing him. Another knocked a calabash of palm wine from an usher's hands. Each time a dancer fell into trance another woman led her out of the arena. I don't know what sort of treatment they received outside my vision, but they eventually returned to the arena fully recovered from their fits and continued dancing.

I found the trances profoundly disturbing. In the West we seek to exert complete control over our physical selves. The body is both the temple and the cult itself. We exercise. We diet. We medicate at the first whispers of rebellion, refusing even to cede authority to aging and disease. We display our victories with pride, and hide our failures under loose sweaters and vertical stripes. Our flesh is under our jurisdiction, marches on our orders, surrenders to no one.

In front of me these dancing women abdicated their bodies to the unseen and bid spirits to commandeer their flesh. They celebrated their bodies' vulnerability. I only wished I knew the reasons why. There were forces at work I can never know, and desires I cannot understand.

After about an hour the drumming stopped and the dancers, senses restored, left the arena. It was time for the unveiling of the sacred stone. First, calabashes filled with palm wine were passed around the audience while a few spectators—dignitaries of some kind—received grass garlands to wear around their necks. A Guin holy man took the stone in his hands and walked around the arena showing it to the crowd. Everyone cheered wildly when they saw its colour and began to dance in their seats. I stretched my neck to see the stone. It was white and looked like a bar of soap.

The man next to me jumped up and began clapping his hands. I asked him the significance of the colour white.

"White is the best colour the stone can be. It means that the Guin will enjoy much prosperity. The Guin will have a good harvest, good rains, good everything."

"Happy New Year," I said.

I returned to the community centre where I was staying and found my quiet street transformed into a block party. Hawkers selling fried yams, roast chicken, chewing gum and cigarettes lined the road. Candles on the vendors' stands and glowing charcoal grills accented the Christmas lights strung from trees. Music charged out of a dozen cassette players and people were dancing and milling in the street. The community centre itself hosted a dance party complete with DJ, enormous speakers and disco lights. I gave up all designs for sleep.

The *fête* centred around Chez Nous, a normally quiet drinking bar across the road from the social centre. A severe Togolese woman called Mama ran Chez Nous with her two teenage daughters. With my room only a few steps away, I was a familiar face at Chez Nous and spent much of my days tottering on the tall bar stools, writing letters home and drinking enough Awooyo brand beer to float a king's ship. Much as I tried, Mama wasn't interested in conversation, preferring instead to treat me with grudging politeness. On the night of the *fête* Mama had no time to chat anyway; the mob of young patrons kept her busy refilling gin glasses and fetching bottles of beer and soda.

I occupied my regular stool at the end of the bar and drank beer while Mama chased away a drunk teen who was pestering me to buy him cigarettes. Looking around the bar I felt both uncomfortable and at home. The afternoon's ritual in the arena was alien and disturbing, but the night's festivities at Chez Nous were almost as shocking in their familiarity; this party could happen in any city in the world. The stereo played nondescript North American hip hop at an aggressive volume, and the only people in African attire were Mama and myself. The place smelled of every dance bar I'd ever been in: a blend of cigarette smoke, grainy deodorant, mint gum and sweat. Young women in tight jeans and tight T-shirts gathered in tight circles. "Look-at-me" girls danced provocatively but alone, and pushed away the men in phony Adidas shirts who tried to press up against them. Drunk men in sunglasses and matching turtlenecks planned clumsy seductions as they chain-smoked cigarettes. The day's ritual was ruled by spirits, the night's by drunkenness and sex. It saddened me that only the latter were forces I understood. If given the choice between African faith and Western-style vice, I would rather be filled with magic than emptied by alcohol and lust.

Benin

Is it a sign of ingenuity or madness that I have started using pages out of my Lonely Planet *for toilet paper?*

I was six months into my journey when I crossed the border into Benin and made my way to Ouidah, a town on the southern coast.

"You chose a good time to visit Ouidah," my guide, Marc, told me as I threw my backpack down in his uncle's hotel. "Next weekend is the Feast of the Twins and tomorrow a family is raising the dead."

There is a voodoo museum in Ouidah, but there doesn't need to be. Temples devoted to the gods of tigers, smallpox and rainbows—among other things—share street space with hairdressers and tailor shops. T-shirts hide torsos marked with ritual scars and tattoos. In the marketplace, magic talismans and dead birds are sold alongside bags of laundry detergent and cooking oil. In one corner of town a Catholic cathedral and the Temple of Pythons stare at each other across a dusty road, competing for souls.

As a regular part of his tour, Marc brought me to see Daagbo Hounon Houna, the Supreme Chief of Voodoo. He lived in a compound that smelled of chicken blood and was littered with animal skulls. Images from a colour television set flickered. He invited me into his living room and sat on a green sofa. I offered his excellency a bottle of gin, along with a cash donation, and he promised to pray to the voodoo spirits on my behalf.

"What do you wish?" he asked.

"I want good fortune and safety for the rest of my travels."

"Is that all?"

I nodded.

"The path will open up before you," he said. He shook my hand and gave me his business card. I walked out smiling with the knowledge that I'd just lubricated Benin's voodoo tourist industry.

Raising the dead, however, was a far less overtly commercial enterprise. After a dinner of fish and rice and over a couple glasses of gin Marc explained the tradition. There is a particular cult in Oudiah that honours their members' dead ancestors by bringing them back to life once every year. All families within the cult engage in this tradition, though usually not at the same time. A room in each family's house is reserved for a mysterious ceremony that involves prayers and sacrificial offerings. Once the ritual is completed, the ghosts of the ancestors, known collectively as Agoun, magically appear and wander out into town for the day.

"Can you can see them?" I asked.

"Oh yes. They walk on the street."

"Do they look like regular people?"

"No. They are different. Tomorrow you will see."

Marc met me the next morning after I finished my breakfast.

"The Agoun will come out late in the day," he explained and took me on a tour of the town to pass the time. We visited a sacred forest decorated with statues of various deities, many bearing enormous phalluses. We also walked the Road of Slaves to the beach, tracking the route slaves were forced to march on their way to the European boats that waited off shore.

Eventually Marc announced, "It is time. We will go looking for the Agoun."

We didn't have to look long. As we turned down a side street,

Marc pointed to a colourful creature moving towards us along the road.

"You see! There is one of the Agoun."

The Agoun was completely covered in layers of bright pink-and-yellow coloured cloth. It wore a red hood over its head and a veil of small white shells hid its face. Its hands were wrapped in coarse cloth. A male attendant accompanied the Agoun; it was his responsibility to guide it around town.

"Who is inside the costume?" I asked, surprised to find myself whispering.

"There is nothing inside," Marc smiled. "It is an Agoun, like a ghost."

"You're telling me that there is no person in there?"

"No. It is a spirit. Maybe it is an uncle in the family, or a grandfather. Somebody who has died. An Agoun. He is coming to us. You will see."

The Agoun spotted us and lumbered in our direction. I could hear it growling a little as it approached.

"He is coming to you." Marc was getting excited. "You can talk to him, but do not touch him."

"Why not?"

"If you touch an Agoun, you will die," Marc said, casually.

"What?" I was suddenly concerned.

"It is true. If a woman touches an Agoun, she will die instantly. If a man touches he will be very sick for five days, then he will die. So don't touch him."

"Do you know of anyone who has died this way?"

"Yes," Marc said flatly. "Many."

The Agoun came right up to me and growled. I smiled and took a half-step back. Then, to my surprise, the Agoun sang me a song:

> *Yavu, yavu, bon soir.*
> *Ca va bien?*
> *Merci.*

This was the song that local children sang to foreigners when they saw them on the street. I laughed at this, expecting something more sinister and less French.

But the Agoun growled again and held out a cloth-covered "hand."

"What does he want?"

"You must give him some money. This is the tradition. They walk in the street and take donations for the family."

I extracted a coin from my pocket. Marc instructed me to drop the coin on the ground and let the attendant pick it up. That way I wouldn't risk an accidental, but deadly, touch. After I did this the Agoun mumbled something to Marc in the local language.

"He wants you to give him some paper money. No coins." Marc translated.

"Sorry, but tell *Monsieur* Agoun that all I have today are coins."

The Agoun seemed satisfied with this and continued along the street.

Marc and I wandered through Ouidah looking for more Agoun. We came across four of them, each dressed in similarly bright costumes and demanding coins from passersby.

After a while Marc led me to a clearing in the middle of town where a large crowd had gathered. In one corner, a group of bare-chested musicians drummed wildly, filling the afternoon with wonderful pulsing rhythms. Marc arranged for a couple of plastic chairs to be brought to us, and we took our seat at the edge of the square. Everyone anticipated the arrival of the Agoun, and the purpose of the drumming was to lure them to the clearing.

When the Agoun finally appeared, the crowd roared and the pace of the drumming increased. There were six Agoun in all. Now in a group, the vibrancy of their colourful costumes was even more pronounced. One had a long green-and-pink cape that dragged on the ground behind him. Others were covered in so many layers of thick cloth that they seemed like animated carpet heaps. Sequins shone in the muted late afternoon light, and as they passed close to me, I could hear the clattering of shells over the song of the drummers. The Agoun shuffled into the centre of the clearing surrounded by the crowd that was now swaying to the music.

Then the Agoun began to dance.

They moved slowly at first, matching the movements of their audience. Then, in time with the fast rhythms of the drummers, the Agoun began to spin, step and shuffle. Each had its own signature dance. The green-caped Agoun rotated its body in time to the music, and its cape picked up the momentum and spun like a pinwheel in the wind. Another was prone to performing acrobatic flips, sometimes landing split-legged on the ground. The "bulkier" Agoun were happy to just shake in place to the music, or charge across the clearing raising clouds of dust. One of the "female" Agoun was less popular. She simply waved her arms in the air and swivelled her hips; not so impressive compared to one who bounced around the square doing backflips. Considering each Agoun was laden with heavy costumes, their dexterity and free-flowing movements were amazing, and the crowd showed their appreciation by shouting, dancing and tossing money into the square.

But the most riotous excitement came when some of the Agoun spontaneously charged out of the clearing and into the crowd. Knowing that a touch from the Agoun spelled death, the crowd scattered, often knocking over chairs and small children in their flight. It became a game after a while, a deadly version of tag, and as the crowd fled the charging Agoun, their faces betrayed both amusement and terror. I remember looking around me to determine the most obvious escape route in case one came racing in my direction, which, thankfully, never happened.

One of the Agoun did finally approach me, but only to ask for money. This time, feeling brave, I placed the coins in the Agoun's "hand" instead of dropping them to the ground. As my fingers came precariously close to touching the Agoun, I sensed the crowd around me become nervous. Marc disapproved and shook his head at me. I never actually touched the Agoun. Daring is one thing, but I was not about to mess with the ghosts of the dead.

After an hour of dancing and drumming, the Agoun left the clearing and wandered back into town. Marc told me they were going "home," back to the special room in their family's house that acts as the doorway to the spirit world. But they would be back next year, growling and dancing in the streets of Ouidah.

It is no wonder that in spite of the best efforts of Christian missionaries, these ancient religions persist. For its final prize, Christianity offers a vague version of the afterlife: streets paved with gold, eternal peace and other ambiguities. The angels spend eternity floating on clouds and metaphors. But the Agoun return to their family and their village every year. And dance.

Aside from touching Agoun, Marc warned me of other actions that might tempt misfortune and are best avoided. Whistling after dark is bad luck, as is singing funeral songs when there is no funeral. And do not look in a mirror when it is raining. If you are walking along the street and are about to pass two people walking together, never walk between them. This is sure to anger the spirits. It is also rude.

My favourite, though, was a taboo associated with bathing. If you are about to wash your hair and you put soap on your head, you must immediately go to the bath. If you do not do this directly, and you stub your toe on your way to the bath, you will suffer bad luck.

"Isn't stubbing your toe bad luck enough?" I asked Marc.

"No. It could be much worse."

The next weekend I celebrated twins.

The annual Feast of Twins was held under the towering trees of a coconut plantation in Zoungbodji, a village along the slave route from Ouidah to the beach. For the Ewe people in Southern Benin, Togo and Ghana, giving birth to twins is one of the greatest blessings the gods can bestow. Expectant mothers give offerings and prayers to the Twin gods in the hopes their children come in twos. (This is much different than the Ewe people just a few kilometres north who regard twins as the ultimate misfortune.) The Feast of Twins is a sort of Thanksgiving celebration. It is an opportunity for families who have been blessed with twins to pay their respects to the gracious gods.

The celebration began with a small ceremony of devotion at the shrine of the Twin gods. Marc brought me to the shrine, but as an outsider, the mechanics of the ritual could not be revealed to me. I was forbidden to watch the devotees and wasn't allowed to approach the altar of the fetish. There was another white man, a British tourist, who pointed a video camera into the faces of the celebrants and onto the fetish itself. His presence, while an irritation to some, was tolerated and the penitents did nothing to shoo him away. I asked Marc why this man was allowed to film such a secret ceremony.

"He paid someone a lot of money," Marc said. So much for the sacred.

The ceremony itself consisted of prayers and the offering of sacrifices of *sodabe*—a potent local liquor—beans, kola nuts and spices to the twin fetish. Leftover offerings were given to those present, and I was permitted to sip gin from a communal glass and to chew a crumb of bitter kola with the faithful.

After the ceremony I walked out of the temple into a bizarre world of doubles. Under the field of coconut palms stretched a strange landscape of picnic blankets and identical faces with identical smiles, bodies dressed in identical clothes. Some of the picnickers carried odd wooden dolls possessed, I was told, with the spirits of their twin siblings who had died. I stepped around the blankets in amazement. Considering these people represented only a few small villages in the surrounding area, the number of twins was staggering, almost creepy. Even more unbelievable was the number of triplets; I counted four sets of blessed threes. I met one woman whose siblings included two pairs of twins and a set of triplets. She was a twin herself and had given birth to twins. She warmed when I told her that she was a very lucky woman. "Yes," she said, her face glowing under a green-and-pink head scarf, "We are blessed." Can science and mathematics explain this, or does the answer lie in the grace of generous gods?

Each twin family brought a quantity of food or drink to the event to share with the other feast goers. Some brought oranges, pots of fried yams or bottles of local gin. One wealthy family had cans of cold Heineken. The gifts acted as a sacrifice to the Twin gods in thanks for their generous blessing.

Most of the adults gathered around the picnic areas of their friends and relations. Especially popular were the families who were giving out gin. The children, on the other hand, rushed from family to family in large noisy groups to collect as much loot as they could. Each time a cloth was pulled away to reveal a new pot of yams or a box of biscuits the children mobbed the offering family. The children were in such a frenzy that often a member of the family wielded a large stick to playfully beat off the invading hordes lest his family be trampled. The action was chaotic but festive, and reminded me a bit of Halloween. The children didn't care what they received as long as they received something, and it wasn't rare to see toddlers share a can of beer or a five year old grimacing as he sipped a cup of *sodabe*.

The noise was seductive and I asked Marc why the adults didn't participate in the action.

"When I was a boy I went crazy like these *petits*. But now I am a man. Now I visit with my friends and maybe have some gin or kola." He waved his arm towards a crowd of children who, with beans spilling out of their pockets, were fleeing the range of another angry stick. "This is for the young."

"I never had a chance to do this when I was a boy." I said.

"No. Where you come from things are very different." Marc looked at me and read my grin. "You want to run with *les enfants*?"

"Yes. Very much. Would that be okay?"

"It is fine for you. You go."

With Marc's blessing I joined a mob of revellers as they swarmed past. Some of them laughed and pointed me out to their friends, but most were too focused on their next score to notice me at all. While Marc shook his head at me—a "crazy" white man among African boys—I raced with the mob from twin family to twin family in a frenzied bid for loot. Even as a novice I managed to stay clear of any swinging sticks. Some of the families regarded me with suspicion, and a few asked me to pay for the offerings, but most were happy to see a stranger immerse himself in their annual joy. An hour later I returned to Marc, out of breath, after scoring a bottle of Coke, a plate of biscuits, a pile of fried yams, a Heineken, two mangoes, a glass of *sodabe* and a pocket full of beans.

I tried to take photos but, for the most part, was told to put my camera away. Some people were suspicious that I would sell the photos as postcards. They didn't want anyone to profit from their faces. One man would not let me take a picture of his wife because he was convinced that I would publish it in a magazine back home.

"When Canadian men see her beauty they will come to Benin to steal her away from me."

I thought this was sweet, in a strange and paranoid sort of way. Other people would not tell me why they refused and simply waved my camera away angrily. In a culture where the smallest personal relic—like a bit of hair or fingernail—could be used by an enemy to conjure up a curse, I understood why someone would be reluctant to surrender their image to a stranger.

As we were leaving the coconut grove we were stopped by a local man, his eyes reddened with alcohol and his speech slurred. He asked me why I was there.

"I am here for the Feast of Twins."

"Are you a twin?"

"Of course," I lied.

"Where is your brother?"

I put my hand on Marc's shoulder. "This is my twin right here."

The drunk man looked confused. "That cannot be true. You lie."

"What do you mean?"

"Because you are a white man, and your brother is black."

"That is because my mother was a white woman, and my father was a black man."

He regarded my claim in a moment of blurry concentration. "Is that true?"

"Yes, of course. Can't you see our faces are the same?" said Marc, joining the joke.

The man walked away mumbling "*Au revoir, Jumeaux Mal.*" Goodbye, Wrong Twins.

As I looked back at the feast, I noticed one pair of twins that I had seen earlier at the picnic. They were identical women, but one wore a traditional patterned dress and head cloth while the other was clad in Western clothes: jeans and a tight red T-shirt. Her clothes betrayed a fit body underneath.

"She is very beautiful," I said offhandedly, pointing in her direction.

Marc lit up at this. "That girl? I know her. Her name is Monique. If you like her we will go to her house tonight."

"I just think she is pretty, Marc. We don't have to go to her house," I said, suddenly nervous.

"That is okay. We will go tonight. She has a cousin who I like very much, Linda. Tonight we will go, and I will have Linda and you will have Monique."

I decided to hold off my objections in the hopes that after a couple of beers Marc would forget about his plan. I wasn't interested in "having" her. Before leaving Canada I made rules about this sort of thing—the sort of rules inspired by integrity and HIV. I didn't travel to Africa to have sex with locals.

But Marc didn't forget, and once darkness fell, I found myself following him to Monique's house. I knew Marc thought I'd jump at the chance for sex with a local girl—as part of the tourist experience—and he was just being a friend and a good guide. These were not my intentions and it felt wrong to be going to her house, but I didn't turn back. Part of me wanted to see how the West African sex and social scene played out. Here was a cultural phenomenon that my guidebook neglected and a window most travellers do not open. So were these anthropological urges I was following, or urges of another kind?

Monique received us lukewarmly. After finding us chairs she promptly headed towards the kitchen to prepare us food. While she was gone Marc kept passing me knowing winks and grins that I pretended not to see. Monique returned with a plate of fried yams and her cousin, whom she had dragged out of bed. The two girls sat on the ground in front of us while Marc worked his seduction and I ate yams. Marc's small talk consisted of: "Linda, what kind of music do you like?"; "Linda, do you like the yams that Monique cooked?"; "Linda you are not talking. Are you feeling fine?" Linda was utterly bored by Marc, and responded to his advances with all the passion of a fried yam. It was all she could do to keep her eyes open and I guessed she would have been happier if Monique had let her sleep. Monique and I didn't say a word to each other. I didn't even look at her, opting instead to kept my attention focused on my food. Clearly Marc was getting nowhere near "having" Linda, and if I kept up my strategic rudeness, I wouldn't be having anyone either. I started to relax.

Suddenly Marc turned to me and said, with some alarm, that Monique's older brother would be arriving home soon and that we had to leave. Excellent. I stood up to say my relieved goodbyes, but Marc whispered to me, "Do not worry. We are all going back to your hotel."

We walked through the dust of Ouidah to my hotel. Marc and Linda walked far behind, leaving Monique and I to continue our non-conversation alone. I had nothing to say, but the silence was embarrassing. I pointed to Monique's earrings, which were in the shape of the letter B.

"What does the B stand for?"

"I don't know. My mother gave them to me." That was it.

At the hotel we drank Cokes while Marc continued to work his charm on Linda. She was unresponsive. Monique and I remained silent.

"You look tired," Marc said to Linda. "Would you like to lie down?" Linda nodded, barely, and Marc led her off to an empty room. He returned a minute later and winked at me. "She's in bed. That is the first step," he whispered.

I wondered why he bothered to return to the table at all. I guess he wanted to finish his Coke. When he was done with his drink he pulled me aside.

"Marcello, you must relax. Play it cool. You will have her tonight. No problem." I guess he interpreted my discomfort with Monique as pessimism. He wanted to reassure me.

"It's not that, Marc, but this is very strange to me. This is not how these things work in Canada."

He smiled. "Don't worry. She will fuck you."

"Maybe she will," I stammered, "but I just don't do this sort of thing."

"Oh, this will be your first time—"

"Of course not," I said with excess bravado.

Marc, not understanding my objection or even really acknowledging it, changed the subject. "Can I have two condoms?"

I grabbed the condoms out of my pack. Crossroads provided three condoms with packets of lubricant in our medical kit. Also included were six sterile hypodermic needles. Apparently Crossroads thought it was twice as likely I'd be sick and would need an injection than I would have a little romance. I handed two condoms to Marc who quickly thanked me and ducked into the room where Linda apparently lay waiting. That left me alone with Monique. I didn't know what to do or say, so I stood up and went into my own room. Monique followed me, silent, and closed the door behind her. She looked around and fingered the mosquito net that hung over my bed.

"*Qu' est-ce que c'est?*"

I didn't know the French word for "mosquito" so I waved my arms like an idiot and made buzzing sounds until she nodded her understanding.

I sat on the bed. Monique took off her clothes and went into the shower. I got up to hand her soap. From behind the white veil of my mosquito net I watched her shower, her skin slick and shining in the weak glow of a single light bulb. I watched as she turned under the water. I watched as she rubbed soap on her beautiful naked body. I watched as she stepped out in front of me, dripping and unsmiling, and lay wet next to me. I could smell her unfamiliar flesh under the scent of cheap white soap. I touched her with the back of my fingers, my head spinning. I didn't know what else to do. She rolled on to me, and I surrendered to what seemed inevitable.

She left in the morning. The sun oozing through the window had made our closeness sticky and uncomfortable. She didn't say a word. I doubt she remembered my name.

I never intended this to happen and I didn't want to think about it. I didn't want to admit that beneath my painted integrity and altruism I wanted it to happen. I wanted an African girl. I thought it was sexy and exotic. I felt ashamed. I felt like a racist and I fled Ouidah that morning, hoping to forget her like I hoped she'd forget me.

It was not yet noon when I arrived at the Lokassa taxi park, but the day was already sweating. I was on my way east to Lake Aheme but traffic on the road was light. I was in for a long, hot wait.

I watched a beggar boy at the taxi park. He was about sixteen years old with torn clothes and a crudely shaved head. He walked through the taxi park with strange jerky steps that kicked up red dust and dyed his bare feet copper. He was a baggage handler, and his eyes seemed panicked as they watched for arriving cars. The boy ran from vehicle to vehicle, hovering over their trunks in case there was a bag inside he might carry. When a trunk opened he grabbed the heaviest bag he saw and lugged it out with his spidery arms. Then, finding the owner, he held out his palm, hoping a few coins might find their way there. They rarely did.

He received scoldings, mostly. Most passengers didn't want help with their bags and the boy was considered a nuisance. Sometimes the drivers themselves shooed him away, but the boy retreated just beyond their angry reach. Other times, it was as if the boy was invisible and passengers pushed past him, ignoring his dirty frame and desperate look. Avoiding his eyes.

Once, when the park was empty of vehicles, a woman selling stew at a nearby market stall called out to him. She gave him a small bowl of plain white rice. The boy shovelled the food into his mouth with his hands until another car rattled into the park. Then he rushed to work, spilling his rice in the dust.

I spent a few days visiting the area around Lake Aheme and the town of Bopa. I sat on the bank of the lake, leaned against a coconut palm and scribbled letters home on thin blue paper. A dozen village children were on the sand in front of me, staring while I wrote. They sat quietly, fascinated by my presence and the scratch of my pen. Each time I turned a page, or shifted even the tiniest bit, they whispered to each other or giggled. When I looked up at them to catch their gaze they quickly turned away, embarrassed, pretending they hadn't been watching.

Eventually my audience abandoned me for the cool joy of the water. In an instant the children shed their clothes—the older ones helping their younger siblings with troublesome T-shirts—and dove into the murky lake. The older boys wrestled with each other, trying to grip brown limbs slick with water. Girls splashed at them and tormented younger brothers by pushing their heads beneath the surface. Someone flung a broken sandal into the broil and a game of catch began. From a distance the midday sun made diamonds on the water and the wet children shone.

Near them an ancient woman bathed, seemingly oblivious to the children and to me. She was naked from the waist up and slowly lifted cupped hands of water to her shoulders, her breasts, her toothless mouth. The woman passed a bar of soap over her aged body. White bubbles drifted from her to the frothing youth, and disappeared in their play.

There was no hotel or guest house in Bopa, but I found accommodation in a dark room with a straw mattress located behind a *buvette*, a drinking bar. I took my meals—usually fresh fish and *pâte*—on the terrace while trying to explain to curious locals why I would ever want to visit this place.

In the early mornings Lake Aheme wears a thick robe of mist. The fog slips off the water's surface and wraps, spirit-like, around the empty stalls of the lakeside marketplace. Clouds hang low around the village. I rarely saw mornings this early but one day I hired a guide to take me out on his *pirogue* for a sunrise tour of the lake.

Bopa was different when the day's heat was just a promise. Shouting children and market ladies were still asleep, and the gentle sound of the water lapping against the boat was the only conversation. Colours, garish at midday, waited, subdued. Aside from the mild fishiness that perfumes all lakeside villages, a few early morning fires lent the only fragrance to the air. These were easier hours, before the air hung thick with sun and smell and noise.

Hounje, my guide, was anywhere between forty and seventy years old. He was slender but muscular, like he was carved from a tree branch, and ritual scars decorated his chest and arms. Hounje poled the narrow, shallow-bottomed boat across the lake. Surprisingly, he let me photograph him and posed proudly at the bow of the boat: yellowed smile and bright pink shorts.

"You send me picture," he said after the click.

By the time the morning sun and the sounds of the waking village had penetrated the mist, we were halfway across the lake, silently slipping to the other bank and the village of Dékanmè, where Hounje was born. Hounje took me on a quick tour of the village. His energy, especially considering the long push across the lake, was startling, and I fell out of breath trying to keep up with him. Hounje led me to many of the holy sites in Dékanmè, stopping frequently to introduce me to his countless relatives. The village was filled with fetish temples. Many had brightly painted exterior walls that contrasted with the dark interiors I was forbidden to enter. One building was devoted to a renowned healer whose specialty was broken bones. On his temple wall were murals depicting his remarkable skills. The first showed a man with a compound fracture on his leg, the broken bone protruding through a gash of torn and bleeding flesh. In the next, the healer put his hands on the injured man, and the third showed the patient walking normally with a perfectly healed leg. I asked Hounje if the healer, his uncle, is a doctor.

"Yes, but not like doctors in the West. He is better."

Several of the temples were filled with sculptures Hounje called *assin*. The sculptures were composed entirely of metal, most often with sheets of tin but sometimes with objects like bolts, gears and car parts. They looked strangely avant-garde, especially surrounded by mud-walled houses and Hounje's naked cousins. Members of a certain fetish cult build the *assin* to honour the ongoing spirit of a dead male ancestor; after death, a man's spirit resides in the *assin* his family builds for him. Respectful family members give regular offerings to the sculptures; I saw kola nuts, piles of cooked beans and small glasses of gin placed at the base of several *assin*.

"Why beans?" I asked. Hounje said the dead get hungry too.

On our way back across the lake I watched two fisherman, working from a small boat. They laid out a large circle of nets under the water. Then, as they piloted their craft around the perimeter, the men worked to frighten a catch into the nets. One man swung a long pole with a weighted end over his head and brought it crashing down into the water. He did this over and over again, using the strength of his entire body to bring the heavy end down with force. The other man had a pair of drumsticks and rattled loud rhythms on the side of the boat in hopes that fish would flee his music and trap themselves in the net. Occasionally the men paused to dive underwater to check on the catch. Unsatisfied they climbed back into the *pirogue* and continued their noise.

Later I watched immortals dance. I joined Hounje in a visit to another village near Bopa. A ritual was to take place that night involving dancing ghosts. On the way we stopped to collect another one of Hounje's uncles. When we entered his house the uncle pulled an envelope from under a pile of papers next to his bed. He swept off the dust and smiled as he placed them in my hands. He had been a soldier in the Beninoise army and the envelope contained his old service records. He sat next to me and explained each document.

"You see? I was a soldier for a very long time." He smiled at a letter of commendation, and pointed to a picture of a much younger man on an old identity card. "That is me as a young man. You see? A proud soldier. A very strong man."

He boasted about his career and his role in *la revolution*. Afterwards he asked me if he could find work in Canada as a night watchman or as a housekeeper, washing floors for white people.

Uncle spent a quarter-hour smearing cream on his chest and dragging a black comb over his hair. Then he led us to a small clearing near the lakeshore where about a hundred villagers were gathered. On the edge of the clearing was a large temple with bright blue walls and paintings of strange creatures that resembled coloured haystacks. Everyone stood staring at the temple, some casually swaying to the music of drummers, all anticipating something I couldn't guess. Three chairs were fetched for Hounje, Uncle and myself and we sat facing the blue temple. After some time three creatures emerged from the temple doors.

"You see? You see the dancing ghosts?" Hounje shouted in my ear above the sudden joy of the crowd.

The dancing ghosts were about seven feet tall, dome-shaped and made entirely of what looked like dried reeds. They were not human in form, except each was topped with tufts of long coloured grass—yellow, blue and purple—like bright wigs. One of the ghosts had horns coming from its head, while another had a crown of pink tissue paper. The ghosts began to "dance," shuttling back and across the clearing, at times spinning wildly in place and sweeping up the red dust. Their movements were chaotic, and each had an attendant to ensure they didn't collide with the audience or with each other, or scuttle off into Lake Aheme. On the outskirts children filled trees for better views. Villagers danced and drummed and cheered and sang, thrilled at the appearance of their local immortals.

The dancing ritual went on for several minutes. At one point, a ghost began to shake madly before becoming suddenly still. The crowd grew excited at this. An attendant rushed to the ghost and tipped it over to show the crowd who, or what, was inside. It was hollow and completely empty. The crowd got wild when they saw this—laughing and cheering—and they looked at me to see the stranger's reaction. I smiled and shook my head, astonished. I wasn't expecting that kind of magic, and I don't know under what eerie power those crazy haystacks danced. All I knew is that my Western skepticism took another blow—I was starting to believe in magic.

By mid-September I was tired. I finished travelling through the southern half of Benin. Voodoo rituals and small villages had given way to cities and marketplaces that, for the first time, could not hold my attention. It had been over a month since I'd seen another traveller and I hadn't spoken English with anyone for at least that long. Even the locals were starting to get on my nerves. On the streets of Cotonou I told a persistent street-side blender salesman to fuck off. He snapped back at me, in English, "Go back to your country." For the first time in five months I wished that I could.

For the next two days I travelled the vertical span of Benin. Through the windows of my train and bush taxi I watched as coastal green faded into beige desert, and trees shrunk into tiny thorny bushes. We clunked northward as the sun set, and I held my arms out the train window to catch the breeze the motion made. I was in better spirits. Motion was a comfort. Travelling cheered me.

I boarded my train at the first station in Cotonou and was lucky to secure myself a seat. By the third stop the train was full, and most passengers spent the journey crammed in the aisles. Africans don't travel light: passengers were laden with bulky plastic baggage, sacks of rice and sugar, children of varying ages and chickens (both alive and fried). In the seat ahead of me a man expressed concern about a live chicken that was stowed in a basket above his head. To ease his fears of falling chicken shit the bird was relocated under a seat. The passengers around him giggled: the hazards of Beninoise train travel.

The voyage from Cotonou to Parakou took nine hours, and the train seemed to stop in every village along the route. At each station, local market ladies mobbed the train selling green-skinned oranges, small smoked fish, bread, groundnuts, tiny bags of ice-water and other provisions. The vendors were not allowed on board so all transactions were done from the train windows. As ladies held up their wares and shouted out prices, passengers crowded in front of each window, holding out cash and trying to get the attention of the vendor they wanted. The train remained at each station for only a couple of minutes, so there was a noisy rush to buy before pulling away. Without fail, the train would start moving before all the transactions completed. Many times, as the train inched forward, I watched a market lady run after the hand waving the money she was owed.

The train journey ended in Parakou where I spent the night before catching a taxi to Malanville on the Niger border. My hotel turned out to be a brothel filled with English-speaking prostitutes from Nigeria. I enjoyed chatting with them, but when they realized I was not buying, they moved on to more lucrative tables.

I left the hotel and went for a walk through town. When I stepped into the marketplace, any residual fatigue and ill mood I carried dissolved. I could hardly believe the faces I was seeing existed: people wrapped in indigo robes, with skin smooth like coffee and cream, and eyes impossibly grey-green. Men and women were adorned with huge silver earrings, bulky beads and bracelets, facial tattoos and ritual scars. Some carried swords and led herds of goats. In the previous months I shared my breath with pulsing thunderstorms, singing drums, Benedictine monks, voodoo priests, ghosts and dancing girls. But I never saw beauty like this. I never had the breath pulled from my chest by a face. I stared all day long, winded, and the dust and joy made my eyes water.

Niger

It's hard when poverty smiles at you. It's much easier when it scowls.

I remember a beggar girl in Cape Coast. She was lying in the shade on the side of Aboom Road. She was like a pile of sticks, her limbs fleshless and twisted into unnatural bends. She couldn't walk, she could scarcely lift her head, but she smiled at me and told me welcome. Laying there in a heap like something discarded and forgotten. And she was so happy to see me she somehow found the energy to smile. Her happiness was as impossible as the angles of her limbs. I think about her often, and I remember how hard it was to smile back at her, and how foolish I felt. She cannot begin to know that her smile hit me like a rock.

Nobody wants to hear stories like that. Everyone wants to hear that the weather is hot and the food is weird and I've learned to wipe my ass without toilet paper. It is easier not knowing about that girl in Cape Coast. I wonder if she is dead now. I wonder how many people remember her.

The truly poor in Africa are difficult to see because they blend in with the rubbish and filth that they live in. They are the moving shadows in the trash heaps, camouflaged in squalor. When you see them the horror is in realizing you are watching them decompose. Their living flesh is slowly being milled into earth, or taken away in tiny flakes by flies. Crawling naked through the trash heaps, they search for bits of food—some wilted lettuce or a banana peel with the little plug of fruit still in the centre. They don't beg. I suppose they haven't the energy. Eventually they just disappear.

On one of my first mornings in Niger, I sat at a taxi park waiting for a ride. I was in the shade with some of the other waiting passengers when a beggar approached me. He was a small naked boy, about three years old, and his left arm was severed from the elbow down. He walked up to me with his one hand extended hoping for a handout. Immediately, reflexively, I shook my head.

But he didn't go away. He stood, rubbing his cheek with his stump, and stared at me with a gaze that I couldn't interpret and cannot forget. He made me feel ashamed of myself. This child with dusty shadows on his bald head, a sticky nose and eyes far too old for him. And me with principles far too clean for this place, far too tidy for this dirty boy and his missing arm. He scolded me by rubbing that smooth stump on his rough cheek. In a moment all that I thought I knew, all my white-man's logic and convictions, all my absolutes, fell into the dust with a clatter only I could hear. And inside me something started to bleed.

Withered, I reached into my pocket and gave the boy some coins. He didn't thank me. He didn't even smile. I didn't deserve it. He walked away, turning back only once with that same punishing glare.

A man sitting next to me saw what had happened. He touched me on the shoulder and handed me a banana.

I made my way to the northern half of Niger to Agadez, where Sahel fades into Sahara. Here, Tuareg nomads still court the sand and, somehow, live off the scarce gifts of the desert. The Tuareg are an intensely beautiful people, known for their blue robes, long silver swords and liquid grey-blue eyes. They are entrancing to view, yet it is because of them I was warned against visiting here. A Tuareg rebellion that officially ended a few years before left residual dangers in the area around Agadez. Armed bandits still struck occasionally on the highways, stealing vehicles and fuel, and it was unsafe to drive at night. There were rumours of kidnappings and shootings, and a story about a Tuareg festival a few years past when unidentified persons lobbed grenades into a crowd. The residents of Agadez walked quietly, as if to avoid waking further demons.

Tragedy has made the ancient city oddly still. Fears of violence kept most travellers in the safer south. The embassy in Niamey suggested I stay away and American Peace Corps volunteers were forbidden to venture here altogether. Further, the horrors in Algeria meant the aged routes across the desert from the north were rarely used. Trans-Saharan travellers and desert caravans stopped coming.

Thus my Agadez lay waiting, a bit impatiently, for the return of safer times and the desert adventurers that would follow. Red dirt roads were lined with tour guide offices with locked doors. Silver shops shimmered next to empty hotels in the marketplace. Land Rovers sat waiting to be rented by adventuring tourists. At the *marché* I met a man who arranged desert skiing excursions. His shop was full of snowboards and skis—scarred badly by sand—and photos of crazed Westerners skiing on dunes. Everyone had desert jewellery or postcards to sell, or camels ready for desert treks, but nobody was there to buy. Nobody, it seemed, but me, seduced by Saharan dreams and the name of the town itself. *Agadez.* It buzzed from my tongue's tip like a mosquito.

I travelled from Zinder aboard the rusted monster of a state Transport bus. The bus formed part of a military convoy that travelled to Agadez only twice a week and was flanked by machine-gun mounted jeeps—an attempt to avoid potential bandit attacks. For additional security, two armed soldiers were positioned on the bus for the entire journey, one at the front, the other near the back, both embracing assault rifles and chain-smoking harsh African cigarettes.

The voyage was incredible. The highway was less a road than a trail of potholes in sand. We cruised over them at such speeds that passengers regularly bounced about the bus like dolls, and seats that were not attached properly clattered into the aisle. At each bump I knocked my head on the roof of the bus then came crashing down on the metal bar where my seat was supposed to be fastened. Then I searched for my fugitive seat, selected it from the others that had broken and flown off, reattached it and braced myself for the next pothole. This process became something of a game, even for the locals who were used to white-knuckled bus trips.

As we rattled northward I watched a solitary man in blue robes lead a train of camels, slowly and silently, across the sand outside. I couldn't believe that a few weeks prior I thought I was ready to go home.

We stopped at dusk in the village of Aderbissinat. Travelling at night is too dangerous, even with the military escort. All the passengers pulled down their belongings and stretched out for the night on the sand next to the bus. The only lodging was a dark, mud-walled shack with the word "hotel" spray-painted on it. It was simply an empty room where passengers, men only, could sleep on the floor and maybe have some tea. Everyone opted to sleep outdoors, however, and a large sheet was spread out on the ground so that the we did not had to sleep directly on the cold sand. I found a spot to lay down while men passed around cups of tea, smoked cigarettes and listened to radios. At *salat*, prayer call, the men rose from their lounging and extinguished their cigarettes. They kneeled and bowed eastward while praying. I lay in the midst of their devotion feeling oddly foolish for not believing. Although I must have seemed an infidel in these people's eyes, they offered me tea and grins. I felt a part of their brotherhood, bound not by language or faith, but by gender and the morning's destination. Lying on my back, I marvelled at how comfortable I'd become surrounded by strangers.

As soon as I arrived in Agadez and started my walk from the bus station to my hotel I collected a crowd of young children. They followed me through the streets singing demands for pens and *bonbons*. Upon seeing my long hair many of the children called me "*Madame*." I decided to grow my beard again.

The buildings in Agadez are constructed with mud and their colours vary depending on the intensity of the desert sun. Sunset was my favourite time as the mud walls glowed a soft orange. Dusk often found me on the rooftop terrace of the Hotel de l'Aïr, a former Sultan's home that was converted into an expensive and empty hotel. From there I wrote my letters, drank rank but cold Nigérienne beer and watched the sun set over slices of hot watermelon. The Grande Mosqueé is across the road from the hotel; its towering minaret can be seen from everywhere in Agadez, reminding the faithful of Allah's presence and Muslim duty. Poles protrude like spines from the mud-made tower, acting as built-in scaffolding for its construction and repair. I pondered the minaret from the terrace and imagined the spirits of the faithful climbing the spines to heaven.

I hired a local guide to take me on a camel trek into the desert. His name was Ibrahim, and he had a disturbing habit of continually snorting and hacking up parcels of mucus from his sinuses and spitting them on the ground. *Snort. Hack. Spit.* He did this, I calculated, once every eight seconds. In spite of this unrequested symphony of phlegm, Ibrahim appeared to be a good guide, and between his slimy ejections we managed to agree on a fair price.

I met him at his home in Agadez where he and two camels stood waiting. Ibrahim wrapped a *tagelmoust*, a three-metre length of black cloth, turban-style around my head and face. Only my eyes were uncovered. Then he led me to my camel.

Mounting a camel for the first time is terror. Ibrahim pulled my camel clumsily to its knees to allow me to climb onto the wooden saddle. When Ibrahim released the tension on the nose rope the animal sprung up in a three-part hydraulic motion that pitched me forward, backward and forward again. Suddenly I was nine feet above the hard sand, with my stomach midway up my throat. Ibrahim handed me the nose rope and warned, "Do not let go of this." He taught me how to sit forward with my right foot resting on the camel's neck and my left foot on top of my right. He told me how to make the camel move: I must push on its neck with my feet and swing the loose end of the nose rope near its eyes. My camel opened its mouth and gargled loudly. Ibrahim berated me for bringing too much baggage, pointing out the camel's complaint.

But it was Ibrahim's camel that eventually mutinied. After travelling about a kilometre out of town, Ibrahim's camel let out a wet bleat and sat defiantly in the sand. Ibrahim tried to get the animal to stand again but it refused. All of Ibrahim's angry pleading only made the camel more stubborn, and he was forced to dismount and lead it by foot. We walked into the desert for about an hour until we came across two men, friends of Ibrahim, who were headed back into Agadez. Ibrahim explained our camel trouble and they agreed to take the defective animal back with them. Ibrahim assured me that he would be able to get another camel at the Tuareg camp where we would spend the night. In the meantime we would have to double up. Ibrahim pulled my camel to its knees again and loaded it with the balance of our baggage from our absent camel. Then he ordered me to shove over so that we could share the already uncomfortable saddle. For hours I travelled like this, cramped on a wooden saddle with a sinus-troubled camel guide stuffed tight behind me. I don't know who sounded worse, the gargling camel beneath me, or Ibrahim hacking and expelling mucus behind my right ear. *Snort. Hack. Spit.* We plodded and snorted across the landscape until we reached the camp at dusk, stopping only for lunch and a long midday siesta.

The camp consisted of about a dozen dome-like tents built by a community of Tuareg. While Ibrahim chose a replacement camel and smoked with the men, a young boy was assigned to me to show me the *jardin*. He led me to a small plantation where the village grew rough lettuce, wheat and tomatoes. The garden's vibrant greenness was made more intense by the pale sand that surrounded it. The boy showed me the clever well system that supported the garden, and the tiny irrigation channels that led to the separate plots like veins. It was fantastic to see so much growth in a landscape that seemed so desolate and unfriendly. Afterwards he led me to his father's tent where I sipped mint tea while his sister, shy and beautiful, offered to sell me the silver charm around her neck.

The Tuareg possess a hypnotic physical beauty. As I sat close to them I was overwhelmed by it. In my months in Africa I was the subject of countless stares. In Niger, it was I who stared, fixated, into startlingly blue eyes and coffee-coloured faces that were the true wonders of this place. Desert landscapes may have drawn me to the Sahara, but in the presence of those faces, in the gaze of those impossible eyes, the scenery became mere backdrop.

For dinner Ibrahim prepared his specialty, couscous and Maggi-brand seasoning salt, and endless cups of mint tea which we shared with all the men. After dinner we were entertained by a man renowned for his ability to make farting noises under his armpit. He stood in front of us and "farted" proudly along to the music crackling from a radio. The children, thrilled by this grand show, urged me to give the man money as a reward for his musical skills. Instead I reached under my T-shirt and demonstrated my own proficiency with armpit tooting, a skill honed to perfection in the locker rooms of Catholic school. The children cheered and soon I was engaged in an armpit fart duel with a desert nomad under the Saharan sky.

That night Ibrahim and I rolled out blankets on the sand and went to sleep under clear desert stars. Nights are cold in the desert; there isn't enough moisture in the air to retain the day's heat. Thankfully Ibrahim brought two blankets, though he was sure to take the thickest for himself.

At about midnight Ibrahim nudged me awake:

"Wake up. You must give me your flashlight."

"Why? What's going on?"

"The camels have left."

"What do you mean the camels have left?"

"They have left."

Our camels escaped—Ibrahim forgot to hobble them. I handed him my flashlight and the tired little man shuffled off into the moonlit nowhere. Ibrahim returned about twenty minutes later; I heard him before I could see him, his hacking preceding him like fanfare. Finally he appeared, walking slowly, with the two fugitives in tow. Embarrassed, he hobbled the camels securely and went back to sleep.

At dawn, after a breakfast of instant coffee, Ibrahim and I continued our trek. The desert was not how I envisioned it to be. The soft dunes of my imagination were further afield than Ibrahim and I would travel. Instead the landscape was hostile and mesmerizing, and reminded me of the surface of the moon. We plodded across lengths of hard flat sand, disturbed by the occasional thorny bush or patch of rough grass. Passing over a hill we suddenly faced a dramatic wasteland of black and red stone that stretched to the horizon. The land looked charred, as if the sun had scorched the earth. From atop my camel I felt the heat radiate upwards from the black ground. Sometimes we came across a line of green trees growing on the edge of a dried out stream bed; persistent roots found water that retreated underground. We paused to rest in the sudden green while butterflies played about our heads.

At a hostel Halloween party in Zinder—where I bobbed for guavas with the Peace Corps—a volunteer told me about a team of paleontologists working in Niger. She heard a rumour that scientists from the University of Chicago were digging dinosaur bones in the desert near Ingal, a small town west of Agadez. Inspired by boyhood fascinations I set out to find the team when I got back to Agadez from my camel trek.

By happy coincidence I found a partner for my search. I met Sam in the Agadez motor park while I waited for transport to Ingal. He was an American volunteer on vacation from his village in Guinea and was also looking for the paleontologists. He heard about the expedition from a local man in Agadez but knew little about their whereabouts. Our only clue was the town of Ingal—surely there was someone there who could lead us to the dig site.

Once in Ingal we asked locals if they knew where the Americans had their camp. Each person had a different answer, so we went to the local military post for information. A soldier escorted us to the bare office of the *prefé*, the head of the local military detachment. He was a large man in army fatigues and wore his gun-blessed authority on his face in a tight frown. He looked at us with undue contempt and was immediately impatient with our presence in his office.

"What do you want?" he barked by way of greeting.

"We are looking for a team of Americans who are digging for dinosaur bones. We heard they are nearby."

"I know the group," he said. "Some of my soldiers are protecting them." He paused. "Why are they digging up bones? Are bones worth money in America?"

"Not really. They dig them up for science."

This answer sounded suspicious to the *prefé* and I doubt he believed us, but he continued. "The Americans are not near Ingal. Their camp is at Marendet."

"Where is Marendet?"

"It is very far."

"Can we find transport to Marendet?"

"No. There is no road, only a *piste,* a trail in the sand." He dragged on his cigarette. "It is in the desert where the Tuareg bandits live. No cars can go there."

Sam pointed into the yard where a military jeep was parked. A soldier was asleep in the back. "Could one of your soldiers drive us there? In the jeep? We can pay you."

The *prefé* shook his head. "No. It is too dangerous. The bandits attack every day. There is much risk." He pointed his cigarette at us. "You should not go to Marendet. And if you go we will not help you if you find trouble. Understand?" We nodded. He arbitrarily checked our passports and sent us out of the room.

Sam and I decided the only way we were going to reach the American camp was to walk there ourselves. We boarded a vehicle headed south along the highway and told the driver to let us off at the next junction. From there, according to my map, Marendet was a tiny dot about twenty-five kilometres away. Sam and I never discussed the *prefé*'s warnings. The opportunity to live out our dinosaur dreams overcame any vague apprehensions. Besides, I didn't consider myself a likely target for a bandit attack. I had no vehicle, no weapons and little money. My pack contained nothing valuable, just some ratty T-shirts and smelly socks. And I'm Canadian—nobody ever harms Canadians.

As we travelled to the junction our fellow passengers wondered where we were going. We told them we wanted to join the Americans at Marendet.

"They are not at Marendet," one insisted. "They are near Ingal."

His friend disagreed. "No, no. It is not true. You are too late. The Americans went home four days ago."

Another man asked, "Where is Marendet?"

While they argued I spotted a grey Land Cruiser travelling towards us on the other side of the road, headed to Ingal. As it passed I saw dinosaur stickers on its door. Our driver shouted out: "Did you see that car? Those are the Americans you are looking for."

It was disheartening to watch them speed past, but at least we knew they hadn't gone home. We reasoned that the Land Cruiser must be headed to Ingal for supplies. Since we knew the vehicle had just come from the camp at Marendet we figured they must have left fresh tire tracks in the sand. This would make things easy for us. We could find the tracks and follow them into the desert towards Marendet. Further, we probably would not have to walk for long. It was unsafe to travel after dark—and we knew an American paleontology team wouldn't risk a highway robbery—so the Land Cruiser must return to the camp before nightfall. As long as we kept to the tracks we could flag down the vehicle as it returned and ride the rest of the way to the camp. It was a perfectly logical plan.

From the junction the *piste* was easy to find. It extended into the desert from the main highway and, as predicted, we spotted fresh tire tracks carving a path in the sand. It was noon and the sun was oppressive so we wrapped our heads in our *tagelmousts*. With no provisions aside from a few litres of water, a handful of groundnuts and some foul Fulani cheese, we were ill-prepared for the expedition and headed straight into Tuareg bandit territory without a guide or any real directions. Still, I wasn't concerned. I expected a walk of less than three hours before a Land Cruiser rescue and the comfort of a well-funded American expedition camp.

After thirty minutes we found a nomad camp under the meagre shade of a grey tree. The camp was small, consisting of a single tent and a couple of camels. The family was excited to see us approach and invited us to sit. As we shared a bowl of sandy water a woman began to moan dramatically inside the tent. Over her moans, Sam tried to ask our hosts about the paleontologists but they didn't understand. They recognized the word "*Américains*" to which they nodded vigourously, but couldn't give us any information. One of the young boys knew a little French, and he translated for us. He asked if we had any medicine, gesturing to the old man who pointed frantically at his throat and made mock coughing noises. We had none. I asked if we could rent his camels. The boy said he would sell them to us for four thousand American dollars. We declined. Suddenly shy, the boy stopped translating. We sat for a moment in complete confusion as the entire family started feigning coughs, chattering in Tamacheq, and pointing to their throats. The little boy was laughing and the moaning from the tent became louder and louder, making even the camels nervous. We thanked our hosts for the water and hurried away.

Sam had us on a strict marching regimen. We paused for a sip of water every thirty minutes and took a break each hour if we could find some shade. We hardly spoke to each other during our walk. The desert was so quiet it seemed meddling to break the silence with voices. Instead the rhythm of my footfalls in the sand and the sound of my breath in my turban lulled me inwards. I enjoyed the sensation of complete solitude even with Sam beside me. The noise and pulse of Africa had filled my head for months. The gift of the desert was a chance for quiet reflection, a chance for my mind to slow down even if my boots kept plodding forward. My eyes remained fixed on the sand ahead, my gaze only breaking to glance at my watch in anticipation of the next water break or to look behind my shoulder for the vehicle that was never there. There was little else to look at, I suppose. The sand was flat, and the landscape barren save for some miniature and inedible wild melons, the rare skeletal tree or the occasional flash of green where leafy shrubs grew along the banks of dried out rivers.

We hiked for hours, much longer than I planned, and there was no sign of a vehicle or camp of any kind. After about fifteen kilometres we were out of food and nearly out of water. The sun was setting and we realized we would have to spend the night sleeping in the desert. As we laid out our packs on the sand near a grove of trees I remembered the *prefé*'s warnings about nocturnal bandit raids. I knew the danger we were in, and how vulnerable we were, but I never mentioned it. Neither did Sam. Verbalizing the risk would make it more real. We chose to stay close enough to the *piste* that we could see any oncoming vehicle, but far enough away to avoid being run over in our sleep. We laughed morbidly at the irony of being crushed by the very car we hoped would save us. We both knew, I think, that such an accident was the least of our worries. I sat on the ground and tried not to think of the danger we were in.

Then, as feared, a man emerged from behind the trees. He wore the traditional blue robes of the Tuareg, and his eyes stared at us from behind the black turban that covered the rest of his face. As he approached I saw the sword swaying beneath his robes and the silver dagger that hung from his belt. Every story and rumour I heard about bandits and rebels and abductions poured into my head. I froze, not knowing what to do, hypnotized by his swinging blade.

But when he spoke my pulse calmed a little. He talked in Tamasheq, and while we couldn't understand him, his soft voice betrayed no malice. In fact he was smiling at us—I could tell by his eyes. He did not mean to lop off my head or steal my socks.

We introduced ourselves, learned his name was Hadj, and signalled that we had no water. Hadj led Sam into the trees where he had a small camp, a few goats and camels, and a well. I stayed behind in case the truck arrived. Sam returned with a supply of camel-smelling well water. Hadj emerged again carrying a bowl of goat's milk and a rough straw mat; he noticed earlier I was lying directly on the cold sand. We shared the milk and Hadj disappeared into the trees again. He returned a few minutes later with another bowl filled with fresh camel milk. It was sweet and warm and still had a layer of froth on the top. Hadj sat next to us and watched as we drank, making sure we finished, then he went back to his camp. We never saw him again.

Sam and I stretched out under an enormous Saharan sky. I enjoyed the pleasant soreness in my legs and the coolness of the night, and fell asleep as Sam pointed out constellations.

We woke before dawn and reached Marendet just as the noon sun began to burn. We could see the town from a distance. The entire settlement consisted of about a dozen, one-storey buildings; most seemed either unfinished or long abandoned. There were no people in the streets, no roaming animals, no life at all. The cartographer who deemed Marendet worthy of a dot on my map had not been there in a long, long time. I'd never seen a more desolate place. My enthusiasm withered. Marendet was little reward after two days walking, and at a glance we could tell there was no American expedition there.

We walked around Marendet in search of inhabitants, peering into buildings without doors. Finally we found a nomad family camped at the edge of the village. They asked us to sit and gave us water and some cold rice. One woman spoke French, and while she brewed tea we asked her about the paleontologists.

"I know them. The Americans come here often. They come for water. Look, they gave this to us." She held up a plastic bag filled with red and yellow Tylenol. No wonder the mock-coughing man near the highway demanded medicine. The scientists were dispensing pills to the locals.

"Where is the American camp?"

"Not far. They are very close."

I smiled at the continued ambiguity. "Do you know how many kilometres?"

"Not many. Two. Perhaps three," she said, pointing into the desert.

I was relieved. Sam and I logged twenty-five kilometres since the previous afternoon. I was exhausted, and my feet were starting to ache. The last three kilometres would take an hour to walk, so we could afford to rest a while. We relaxed in the shade with our hosts, enjoying the sweet, hot tea and eating our rice with large wooden spoons. In light of our long march these minutes of comfort and hospitality were golden. Even the ragged grass mats we reclined on were a welcome luxury. It seemed ridiculous that we were supposed to fear these desert people.

Energized by tea and rice, and by the knowledge we hadn't far left to travel, Sam and I continued our journey. We followed the Land Cruiser tracks east into the desert. We started at a quick pace, but our enthusiasm quickly evaporated in the day's violent heat. After an hour we found nothing. My pack suddenly weighed a thousand pounds, and one of the straps began to cut the circulation in my right arm, leaving it numb. Further, the soft sand made walking difficult. But we kept going.

After two hours I bent to tie a lace and found the heat had melted the bindings on my boot soles. The leather pulled free from the soft rubber and hot sand filled my boots. I paused to change into my sandals, and shuddered when I pulled the socks off my feet. They were swollen beyond pain, beyond recognition. I thought they might burst. Not knowing whether to cry or scream I didn't say a word.

We kept walking, refusing to quit, mindlessly bold and stubborn in the way only men can be. We stopped more frequently to drink, but our remaining water was too hot to be refreshing. "We could make tea with this," I joked. Many times we heard engines in the distance, or saw vehicles approaching from the horizon, but they were never real, just illusions born of heat, fatigue and stubborn hope. My dead boots hung around my neck and bounced against my chest on every step, trying—I imagine now—to kick some sense into me.

After nearly three hours our water was gone. We stopped. The desert plain was flat and we could see for miles around. There was nothing—no camp, no vehicles, no Americans—nothing but sand in every direction. I looked down at the Land Cruiser tracks which continued to lead us into nowhere and heard them laughing. We turned around, defeated, and began to follow our footprints back.

As the meagre buildings of Marendet grew closer I felt a strange mix of failure and relief.

Upon reaching Marendet we found a large water tank near a cluster of nomad tents we didn't notice before. The tank was mounted on a trailer and decorated with dinosaur decals and stickers from the University of Chicago—this was the water supply for the expedition team. We walked up to the tank, pressed our faces against the cool plastic hulk and decided to steal some water. After two days walking in the desert this was the closest we came to finding the paleontologists. Filling our bottles with some of their clean water would be our small consolation.

As we fiddled with the hose on the back of the tank, a half dozen Tuareg emerged from the tents and marched towards us, each armed like Hadj with a long silver sword. Again I had a brief flash of decapitation anxiety and knew I hadn't the energy to run. One man told us they were hired by the paleontologists to guard the tank from thieves, and he wondered what we were doing in Marendet.

We told him about our two-day trek and how we gave up on finding the American camp. He laughed at us. "But why? They are very close." He pointed into the desert. "Only three kilometres."

I was weary of hearing how close the Americans were, and refused to follow any more pointed fingers into the desert. Considering the ache in my feet I wasn't sure if I could walk at all. As far as I was concerned our search was through. Sam, though, was determined. He noticed a donkey tied to a cart near the tents.

"Will you take us to the Americans? With the donkey? We will pay."

The Tuareg agreed and demanded an outrageous fare. We tried to haggle, but Sam and I knew that two lost, exhausted and nearly lame foreigners had little bargaining power. We agreed on a price, climbed aboard the cart, and rattled off, again, into the desert. We were an odd-looking caravan: a pair of robed Tuareg guides, two turban-wrapped white men and a donkey loaded with blue backpacks. The terrain was difficult and the cart bounced over the uneven sand. Still I may have slept were it not for the repeated thwack of our driver's stick on the otherwise unmotivated donkey.

Our guides led us towards some rock formations south of Marendet, nowhere near our previous route; I wondered where those Land Cruiser tracks would have led. After about eight kilometres we reached the formations and our guides stopped.

"The camp is over there," they said, looking at the rocks.

Sam and I couldn't see anything. "Where?"

"They are close. Just behind those mountains."

"Can you take us there?"

"No."

I waited for an explanation but got nothing. "Why not?" I asked.

"Because the Americans have soldiers guarding their camp. They are protecting against bandits. If they see us coming they will shoot us. You go yourself."

"Won't they shoot at us?"

"Probably not."

It was nearly dusk and we had no time to argue. Our guides were convinced the soldiers would open fire, so they turned around and clattered back towards Marendet. Sam and I removed our *tagelmousts* hoping the soldiers, wherever they were, could tell we were white foreigners and not Tuareg bandits. We strapped on our packs and walked into the mountains where the men had pointed.

We scrambled over the rocks, not knowing if we would find Americans or gunshots. We moved quickly. Once the sun set we'd find nothing, and in darkness the guards would surely assume we were bandits. Still all we found were boulders, and I started to worry.

Suddenly we heard the sound of an engine. We looked behind us and saw a vehicle approach, leading a cloud of sand. At first I didn't believe it was real; we had been seeing and hearing things all day. When it came closer I could see it was a grey Land Cruiser covered in dinosaur decals. It was the vehicle we saw the day before, the one we were waiting for.

We waved our arms like lunatics and the vehicle pulled up

beside us. I rushed up to touch it to make sure it really existed. A turbaned soldier carrying an assault rifle sat in the passenger seat, but the driver was an American covered in plaster dust. He stepped out of the car. He was tall and had a long tangled beard, and I thought he looked like Jesus. He might as well have been Christ as far as I was concerned. He looked down at us and was silent for a moment, as if he wasn't sure if we were real. Finally Jesus spoke.

"What the fuck are you guys doing out here?"

"We're looking for you!" we sang.

"There are bandits out here, you know, and soldiers." He paused. "Are you thirsty?" We nodded feverishly, like children. He handed us his water bottle. The water was cold and flavoured with limes.

"Well, get in," he said.

We jumped aboard the Land Cruiser and drove into the rocky cliffs. The camp was less than a kilometre away, but it was hidden behind a small outcrop of rock. Sam and I would never have found it on our own.

Ten tanned paleontologists crowded around a kerosene lamp eating dinner. When Sam and I came out of the Land Cruiser they put down their plates and stared at us.

"I found these guys in the desert," Jesus announced.

"Hi," I said, too excited and exhausted to sound intelligent.

We introduced ourselves to Paul Sereno, the expedition leader, and joined the others. We told them how we followed a trail of rumours and misinformation forty kilometres into the desert. We told them how we ignored the *prefé*'s warnings about bandits and how we spent the previous night on the sand. We told them about my melted boots and swollen feet and how we stole water from their supply in Marendet. It was only in retelling the story, and watching the others shake their heads at us, that I realized how foolhardy we had been.

Paul let us join the expedition; considering our trek he couldn't turn us away. We met the rest of the team—Jesus was actually J.P.— and finished the remains of their dinner. I slept in the back of the Land Cruiser that night. My feet were swollen and painful, and my face was still streaked with salty crusts of sweat. Still, I felt like a champion. The next day I would dig for dinosaurs.

There was a time for me when nothing mattered but dinosaurs. I remember poring over thick dinosaur books, marvelling at ancient skeletons in museums and somehow memorizing all their delicious multisyllabic names: brontosaurus, tyrannosaurus, pterodactyl. As a child, few topics stirred the blood like giant, long-dead lizards. In Niger's desert, a world away from school libraries and museum field trips, my childhood mania was reborn. Spending days with prehistoric bones, I was the envy of a world of children, and I felt ten years old again.

The expedition camp sat on the foot of the Falaise de Tiguidit, a range of desert cliffs that is a virtual dinosaur cemetery. Ancient bones reached for daylight out of soft rock, or lay directly on the ground as if scattered yesterday. In fact, the team found the skeleton of a young dinosaur by accidentally driving over its protruding spinal column with the Land Cruiser. They dubbed the find the "Road Kill" site, and this is where I laboured for five days.

We woke early each morning, and after a quick breakfast of granola and brewed coffee—Starbucks, no less—we began our work. As a novice I thought Paul would assign me only menial chores: mixing plaster, fetching water, tearing burlap into bandages. But by my first afternoon I joined the others in the pit, chisel in hand. Days were long: aside from a break at noon we worked until dusk. By sunset my arms were coated with plaster and my hair was filthy with dust.

Twilight was stunning. Rocky cliffs encircled us, and at dusk the light reflected off the orange rock, surrounding us with sunset.

Each night, before sleeping, I rubbed my sore arms—not to relieve the ache but to feel it more. The mild pain reminded me of the boyhood fantasy I lived each day in the pit. I worked on my back, chiselled red rock from ancient bones, clothed fossils in white bandages and pulled off my shirt to tan in the morning before the sun became flesh-sizzling hot. I felt cool plaster stiffen on my arms, then felt it melt away in a bucket of filthy water. After lunch I hid from the sun under a Land Rover, napping under its oily mechanics, and felt the cool sand through my T-shirt. At night, by kerosene light, I used a pocket knife to scrape plaster from under my fingernails. Then we turned off the lamp to better see the stars.

Some nights one of the paleontologists, Jeff, entertained the team with miniature gladiator battles. Jeff spent much of his lunch breaks capturing desert insects, and he'd pit them against each other in a small sand coliseum he dug for this purpose. The current champion, an enormous black bug with a fierce temper, dispatched two scorpions, a mantis, a half-dozen dung beetles and a team of angry ants. Jeff kept his champ in a jar beside his sleeping bag. The jar was shut tight to prevent escape and subsequent revenge.

Jeff told me about the soldiers who guarded the camp. They were former Tuareg rebels who, under a government-brokered peace agreement, gave up their weapons in return for jobs in the military and, by extension, better weapons. They spent most of their time sitting under a tree drinking tea and cleaning their guns. Once each day, and with considerable glee, the soldiers "tested" their weapons by firing rounds into the cliffs. In addition to their assault rifles, which they cradled lovingly and never put down, the soldiers had a large machine gun. It was mounted on the back of a pickup truck with a tree branch. Blasting the mountains with machine gun fire was the highlight of their day. They cheered at the racket the way children cheer at firecrackers.

When I first met the soldiers they had a small goat tied to their tree. Eventually they killed and roasted it. They gave the skull to J.P and applauded when he mounted it on the front of the Land Cruiser. But I think they liked Allison best, not just because she was young and beautiful, but because they liked to laugh at her name. Allison sounds like Al Hassan, a common name for Nigérienne men.

In addition to her work in the pit, Allison took charge of the team's provisions. The expedition was outfitted with a ton of dehydrated food and space-age snacks, including a vast supply of Jolly Rancher candy. All the good flavours were gone by the time I arrived; only lemon remained. I enjoyed the novelty of eating beef jerky for lunch and dehydrated chicken chili for dinner, but I stopped mixing Tang into my drinking water. The sugar and chemicals started to give me headaches.

Between bug battles, Jeff told me how fortunate I was to be a part of the dig. Dozens of students from the University of Chicago apply to join Sereno's various expeditions, but only few are selected.

"There were a ton of people who would have given their left nut to get on this trip," Jeff said poetically.

He didn't have to tell me how lucky I was. Sometimes I crawled out of the pit just to stare down at the prehistoric spine arcing in stone, bones millions of years old that I was coaxing free. I couldn't believe I was there.

Eventually my days as an amateur paleontologist came to an end. Once all the fossils were jacketed we loaded them onto a truck, broke camp and drove to Agadez. Sam and I shared beers and one last meal with the team before returning to Zinder. I didn't return empty-handed. On our last afternoon on the dig, while we waited for the truck to arrive, Hans, the team medic, wandered out to do some prospecting. When he returned he pulled me aside and asked, "Would you like a souvenir?" He dropped a small fossil in my hand. It was a tooth. "That is from the same animal as in the Road Kill site. Keep it. Just don't show Paul. He'll want to bring it back to Chicago." I wrapped it in paper and hid it in my sock.

After I returned from the desert, Peace Corps volunteers invited me to celebrate American Thanksgiving with them in Maradi. I shaved for the occasion. The volunteers were excited to have me as a guest—they don't get many visitors—and were interested to hear my stories of the desert and dinosaurs. I felt like a kindergarten teacher telling stories to a rapt audience seated on the floor before me. It was a joy to be the centre of attention in a hostel full of women.

In the midst of my storytelling, chills began to surge through my body. I ignored them at first; I had no intention of letting a case of the shivers interrupt my fame. I wrapped a blanket around me and continued. Within moments, though, I was trembling so badly I could hardly speak. Another moment and my head filled with heat and ache and became so heavy I had to lie down. My flesh was reduced to quivers in a matter of heartbeats.

One of the volunteers took my temperature. She looked confused when she read the result. She shook the thermometer and slipped it back into my mouth. After reading it again she walked out of the room to the others. I heard women discussing my condition above the roaring in my head.

"His fever is forty-one degrees."

"That can't be right. He would be unconscious."

"I checked it twice."

"Maybe the thermometer is broken."

"Let me check it."

Another cold glass tube was pushed under my tongue. After a couple of minutes it left my mouth and the room.

"Forty-one."

"I can't believe it."

"He's burning brain cells."

"It must be malaria."

"I've never heard of a fever that high before."

"What else could it be?"

"We have to cool him down."

The fire raging in my head made the rest of the afternoon a bit unclear. I remember hands unbuttoning my clothes and pressing cold towels on my chest and head. Someone held cold water to my lips. I was embarrassed to be such a bother. Then I felt a woman— she smelled of sandalwood—hold my shaking hands and push a needle into a fingertip. I tried to help her but my limbs weighed a thousand pounds. She squeezed thick red drops onto a glass slide and rushed them to a clinic down the road. I slept and smouldered. I could do nothing else.

When I first arrived in Africa I thought my body was invincible—at least I thought thinking it was would make it so. But when

Sandalwood returned with the diagnosis, it turned out that malaria had found me. Stuborness, clearly, is not a vaccine. She reported that the doctor had never seen blood so sick, so swimming with the parasite. I smiled feebly, like I had won some macabre trophy. Considering the impressive parasite count in my blood sample, I must had been hosting malaria for weeks. The malaise I felt when I first arrived in Niger, headaches I had blamed on the heat, probably had more sinister origins. While I was wandering the desert malaria worms were dividing and slow dancing in my cells. It's fortunate they waited until I was surrounded by Americans and medicine cabinets before starting their hot show. The volunteers gave me a hefty dose of an emergency drug and assured me that by the next morning my fever would break.

As I lay there, delirious with fever, I could picture tiny worms in my cells, twisting inside corpuscles and making my blood hot and thick. I thought I felt them wriggling.

I woke hotter than ever, my temperature still in delirium range. The emergency drugs had failed. The excitement of those around me increased. I heard people in other rooms whispered "cerebral malaria," a killer, and I could do nothing but hope someone knew what to do. The volunteers called their American doctor in the capital who broke a handful of regulations by prescribing me another nasty cocktail of sulphonamides—drugs with a long list of harsh side effects. The Canadian Embassy was contacted and put on alert in case my condition worsened and I would have to be evacuated. It was bizarre, almost comical, to be lying on a floor while a dozen strangers across the country buzzed about in a minor panic on my behalf. It seemed so ridiculous, and I watched, horizontally, as the melodrama wrapped itself around me.

After a couple of hours the second round of drugs brought my fever down for the first time in two days, and the panicky storm surrounding me began to settle. The drugs left me nearly deaf, a rather unsettling but temporary side effect. The next day my health continued to improve, and the Canadian Embassy was put off alert.

Why did I find all this so hilarious?

I've heard stories, warnings, that the parasites will never really leave my veins. I might harbour stowaways in my cells forever, clinging to behind my ribosomes and mitochondria. This is the ultimate intimacy. Tiny natives of the place, Africans, entered me via a drop of mosquito spit and are now part of my basic physiology. What an unlikely new residence for them—red cells cased in strangely white flesh. This is more important than the photos I snapped, more vital than the beads I wore on my wrist or the cowry shells on my neck that warded off demons but not disease. The barnacles in my blood are my most visceral souvenirs. I felt morbidly proud of this.

I recovered from my fever in three days and returned to Niamey. I took a bush taxi from the chaotic taxi park, or *gare,* to Baléyara for the Sunday market. En route our car suffered a flat tire. The driver pulled the lame vehicle to the side of the road and replaced the flattened tire with a spare that seemed equally damaged. Concerned passengers questioned the safety of the spare, but the driver reassured us that everything would be fine. We drove until we reached the next village where the driver stopped again. He removed the spare and brought it to a rough mechanic shop where a nine-year-old boy added air to it with a hand pump, which took about twenty minutes. Afterwards the tire was still soft and worn, and in no better condition than before the "repair." The passengers protested again but the driver confidently reattached the wheel and we carried on towards Baléyara.

After a few kilometres we came upon a horrible wreck on the side of the road. Another bush taxi hung halfway out of the ditch. It was totalled. The front end was mangled from what must have been a head-on collision and all the windows were smashed. The accident must have happened recently—there were still shards of glass scattered over the highway—but the wreckage was deserted. Our driver pulled over beside the wreck, got out of our taxi and peered into the broken vehicle. I thought he was looking for casualties, but instead he pilfered a spare tire from the back. He replaced our problem spare with the stolen tire from the wreck. Afterwards he tossed our spare into the back of the smashed taxi and we continued to Baléyara.

Of all the markets I visited, Baléyara's was the most magical. Looking at the delicate faces of Woodabe merchants, or into the grey eyes of Tuaregs, inspired anthropological yearnings. As I wandered, I saw Zarma women with facial tattoos and pierced noses chat behind piles of sugar cane. A young girl in a frilly dress and brown beads snarled into my camera lens, then giggled and ran off when she heard the shutter click. I saw an old woman with a nasty cough hacking into the grey millet porridge she sold. Under the neem trees a second forest, made of different coloured plastic mats rolled and standing on their ends, was gradually felled by the day's commerce. As I wove my way around heaps of kola nuts and dusty tea, three teenage girls passed, sausage-thick braids with silver clasps hanging out of their headcloths. When I walked by tables of French soaps and perfumes the scent of roses temporarily replaced the smell of sweat and tobacco. Under the shade of dried palms a silent barber shaved a bald merchant. The barber placed his fingers on his client's face to steady his head, pulled his bottom lip upwards with his thumb, then scraped away whiskers with a bit of razor. I watched them awhile and wished I still had a beard to lose.

On the edge of Baléyara was the animal market. The smell was overwhelming and the noise terrific. A thousand animals mooed and bleated while their owners haggled prices. Doomed goats circled corrals made of thorns. Long-horned cattle sat in the dust, seemingly bored by the mayhem that surrounded them. Teenage boys smoked cigarettes and whacked sticks on donkey backs. Flies rioted around the piles of dung I tried to avoid. Hundreds of camels belched and farted and looked witless. As I walked around his herd a camel merchant spotted the camera around my neck and asked me to photograph him. He placed his hand on the side of his most prized beast and frowned into the lens, serious as a prophet.

Other kinds of merchandise were for sale. In one corner of the marketplace was a simple mud shack designated as the market brothel. Vacant for the rest of the week but busy on Sundays, the brothel housed prostitutes from around the region who came to service lusty traders. The prostitutes toured village market days just like the other merchants. I could smell the brothel before I saw it. Thick perfume filled my nostrils long before I passed the women who waved and smiled at me through heavy makeup.

The prostitutes reminded me of a story I heard in Zinder. I met a Peace Corps volunteer who was assigned to facilitate small business growth in her village. After some discussion the elders decided their community would be best served by building and operating a brothel. A house for prostitutes would attract men from the surrounding area, they argued, and this would boost the local economy. They asked the volunteer for help setting up the business and couldn't understand her objections. After all, wasn't that her job?

I roamed the market until noon, when heat slowed trade and merchants sought rest and shade. I watched traders nap beside their stalls or, in the case of the blanket and textile vendors, on top of their merchandise. I took refuge in a small restaurant near the market. I ordered a Fanta and the proprietor brought over an open box of drinking straws. He shook the box so some of the straws protruded out from the others so I could select my straw hygienically.

I asked the man if he had any ice. He scanned the restaurant and noticed a customer about to leave. He had finished his drink but a sizeable chunk of ice remained in his glass. My waiter walked to the table, reached into the glass with his fingers and lifted out the ice cube. Then he dropped the ice into my glass and delivered it to my table.

After spending the night at a Peace Corps hostel where American volunteers, impressed by my stories of malaria and dinosaurs, let me stay for free, I returned to Niamey. Here I sat on the banks of the Niger River to watch the sun set over the water. Rainfall was scarce that year, I was told, and the river moved slowly. If it wasn't for the occasional clumps of vegetation that floated downstream, it would have been difficult to tell if the water moved at all. The slowness of the river and the warm pastel glow of the setting sun was incredibly narcotic. The sky was reflected so perfectly by the near stillness of the water it was hard to tell where the sky ended and the river began. The effect was soothing and otherworldly. And uncertain. Still motion and water sky. The whole world was calm. Even the silver merchants—who have a nose for white travellers, no matter where they hide—were silent. Reverential.

Niamey is Niger's capital and my favourite West African city. I learned to walk slowly there. For days I threaded my way through the red, dusty city streets, fuelled by endless bags of fresh dates and a fascination that had not been this strong since I'd first arrived in Africa over seven months before. Taxis shared the road with camels. A herd of goats caused a traffic jam. The roads were lined with palm trees that provided vital shade from the midday heat. In the shade crowded the date sellers, the meat grills, the old men sleeping or chatting against tree trunks. I watched two boys empty a cow's stomach into an open sewer. The smell was overwhelming: a strange bouquet of wet grass and shit.

In the mornings I watched the meat vendors lay huge pieces of meat on roadside grills. By noon the meat was cooked through and buzzing with flies, and the air filled with the smell of roasted beef, mutton and goat. For a few coins the vendors sliced me off a handful of meat, wrapped in brown paper recycled from sacks of cement.

The market was enclosed by high mud walls, and while there was no roof, market sellers draped cloth over the narrow passageways. The resulting light was surreal: muted colours and the occasional bright flash where the sun charges through a tear in the fabric. I walked through the market corridors the previous day around prayer time. Muslim men squatted outside their booths ritually washing their bodies in preparation for their devotions. I had to move carefully so as not to step in the small pools of water they left behind, their puddles of Islam. Around a corner I entered a clearing underneath the sun where forty men in coloured robes were praying, bowing and kneeling. I suddenly felt like an intruder, an infidel in the face of the faithful. The normal din of the marketplace was replaced for a few moments with the hushed song of Arabic prayers.

By late afternoon the sun had done its work; long shadows muted loud days. And the camels walked out of the plots of romantic dreams and into the red streets. They know how to walk slowly.

The real magic of this place was the people. The Nigériennes exude a beauty born of camel milk and sweet, sweet dates. A beauty fired in a kiln of sun and drought, flavoured by salt and mint, adorned in silver and smoothed by sand. I could not help but stare. I was jealous. I wanted to be that ancient.

Burkina Faso

From December to February the harmattan *wind blows sand and dust from the Sahara Desert into the skies throughout West Africa. It results in a hazy sky, reduced visibility and altered perception; the strange feeling that things are not what they were, or at least not what they seem.*

There is so much I thought I knew before I came here. I knew my mind and its philosophy, my body and its limits. I knew religion but put my faith in science. I knew what it meant to be a white man and a Canadian. There was so much I was certain of and so many lines that I had drawn with a chisel in stone. Now it is not as if the lines have been erased and redrawn. Instead, the stone has turned to dust and has blown away.

I am sure of one thing: The world does not need to be saved, only savoured.

By the seventh month of my travels, I developed a habit of imagining my return to Canada. I pictured surprising my family at Easter dinner, or finding out where Anne worked and arriving unannounced, watching her eyes grow wide and hear her laugh at my long hair. These visions were not accidental slips of consciousness. They were deliberate. Designing elaborate homecoming scenes in my mind became a hobby. In my daydreams I worked out all the details. The open-mouthed shock from my friends. The smart-ass remarks from my uncles about my crazy African clothes. My mother's tears. The friendly welcome embraces. I wondered if I was homesick.

From Niamey I took the state bus across the border into Burkina Faso and its vowel-blessed capital of Ouagadougou. I planted my bags at a downtown hostel and found transport to Sabou where, according to my map, there was a lake populated with sacred crocodiles. The lake was set up as a minor tourist attraction with a rough cement restaurant and a two-room hotel. A guide greeted me when I approached the lake and collected a small admission fee. I started to walk towards the lake but my guide stopped me. "Wait," he said, and walked towards some bushes near the restaurant where a few scrawny chickens pecked at garbage. He grabbed one of the chickens, tied a length of string to its legs then signalled me to follow him to the water.

At the edge of the lake the man swung the terrified bird over his head and tossed it into the water. Soon, a lumbering reptile drifted towards the chicken, and my guide coaxed it ashore. While the crocodile chomped down on the unlucky bird I squatted down over its tail. My guide snapped an obligatory photo. He told me I could sit on the crocodile's back if I wanted; the reptile was distracted by its dinner and wouldn't pay any attention to me. I declined. Once the chicken was messily devoured my sacred crocodile slipped back into the murky water and my "tour" ended.

There was a bus load of four year olds at the lake. They were on a field trip to see the sacred crocodiles. While the children danced, sang and played games in a nearby mango grove I chatted with one of the teachers in the restaurant. I bought him a Fanta in exchange for a seat on the bus back to Ouagadougou.

The children crammed into the bus six to a seat. There were no empty spaces for me so I shared a seat with four toddlers and held one little girl on my lap. As soon as the bus began to move the children started singing "*au revoir*" to the crocodiles in varying degrees of unison. For half the journey the bus rang with the happy disharmony of Mossi songs and French nursery rhymes. Eventually, the kindergarten cacophony faded and children leaned against each other, falling asleep in awkward heaps. The girl on my lap never spoke to me, but she rested her head on my shoulder and slept, trusting that as we bounced over potholes I wouldn't let her fall. Across the aisle a young boy stared up at me. His left eye was clouded by a silver disc of cataracts.

By now *harmattan* season had begun. As we drove back to Ouagadougou, the wind blew dust into the bus windows. It covered each child like a beige veil, gradually muting the colours of their clothes and skin. I watched the dust settle on my trousers until the pattern of the cloth completely disappeared.

When we neared the city the chaperones roused the sleeping children with shouts, and began sorting through the school bags and jackets that were piled randomly at the front of the bus. As we approached the school ground we saw the crowd of parents who were waiting to pick up their children and take them home. One of the teachers commanded, "Your parents are waiting for you. Everybody sing!" She led the drowsy students in song to harvest smiles from the parents as the bus came within their earshot. I thanked the headmaster for the ride, chatted briefly with some curious parents, then caught a taxi downtown.

The next day I visited the Canadian Embassy in Ouagadougou to add more pages to my passport, and I saw a woman in the lobby I thought I recognized.

"Excuse me. Do you speak English?" I asked.

"Yes."

"You look familiar. Were you a volunteer with Crossroads?"

"Yes I was."

Turns out the woman, Olivia, volunteered with Crossroads in Burkina Faso. I recognized her from an orientation meeting in Toronto. She finished her volunteer placement in August and found a job in Ouagadougou. She signed on to a year-long contract teaching English at the American School. I would have loved a reason to stay in Africa. I was jealous.

"Do you have a place to stay?" she asked. I told her I was in a hostel downtown. "You can stay with me, if you want. My roommate, Robin, has a couple of guys staying with us right now, but there's plenty of room. You guys can fight over the couches, if you want." She scribbled directions to her house on a slip of paper. "I have to get back to the school but you can come by any time."

I visited the giant market in central Ouagadougou. Within minutes I gathered a crowd of souvenir sellers that followed me around and tried to draw my attention to their stalls of cheaply made beads, masks and batiks. By the time I reached Burkina Faso I was used to high pressure sales, but the merchants in Ouagadougou were aggressive and rude. Each time I even paused in front of a stall I was mobbed by other sellers who tugged on my shirt and demanded I see their merchandise next. I bought nothing and escaped as my blood started to heat.

I sought refuge in a tiny restaurant down the road, ordered a plate of *fufu* and started to write some letters home. A Burkinabé teenager walked in from the street and sat across from me at my table.

"I followed you from the *marché*," he said. "What is your name?"

"My name is Marcello, but please, I would like to get some work done here if you don't mind."

"Where are you from?"

"I'm from Canada. Please, my friend, could you leave me alone? I am busy."

"Québec?"

"No. Please leave me alone."

"You want to buy postcards?"

A giant woman at the next table stood up and shouted at the man to leave me alone. He stood up, knocked over his chair and shouted back at her. The restaurant owner, attracted by the commotion rushed out of the kitchen, asked what was wrong and promptly kicked the boy out of the restaurant. The postcard boy, on his way out the door, poked a finger in my chest and said, "If I ever see you at the marketplace again I will kill you."

After my meal I took a taxi to Olivia's house. The day's aggravations were getting to me. I wanted to spend an evening in the company of Westerners who didn't want to fight or sell me anything. Olivia lived in a distant Ouagadougou suburb. The taxi ride was long, and as I expected, the driver demanded an extortionate fare. The negotiations for a more reasonable price started friendly enough, but took an ugly turn when two American men, Robin's friends, came out of the house and decided to argue the fare on my behalf. One of them, tall acne-scarred Jeff, shouted into the face of the taxi driver, accusing him of being a thief and a cheat. The driver, not about to be disrespected by a boorish American, shouted back, and before long both were waving fists and spitting insults. Jeff's friend Josh pulled a camera out of his bag and started taking photos of the whole affair.

"This is good stuff," he said.

Further enraged, the driver threatened to smash Josh's camera. Between shutter clicks Josh taunted, "What are you saying? What are you saying? I don't speak French."

The racket attracted Olivia's neighbours who emerged from their homes to investigate the noise. Before long a dozen people were arguing with Jeff, and with each other, over how much I should pay. Jeff spat rage at all of them, obviously enjoying himself. I stayed mute. Everyone forgot about me.

When Olivia finally came outside Jeff was yelling at an elderly Burkinabé woman while Josh leaned his camera in for a close up. Olivia was horrified. I tucked some money under the taxi's windshield wiper and retreated with Olivia into the house. Jeff and Josh continued the battle outside. Eventually the noise subsided and the boys came in.

"That driver is a fucking prick," Jeff said, before introducing himself to me. He was a Peace Corps volunteer.

Despite our chaotic introduction, and the fact that Jeff wanted to pick fights with Africans at the bar that night, Josh, Jeff and I decided to travel to Bobo-Dioulasso together. I would have rather travelled alone, but my finances were starting to thin and I couldn't pass up the opportunity to share a hotel. I only hoped Jeff could keep his temper in check.

I read about Dafora's sacred fish pond in my guidebook and was expecting something akin to the crocodiles at Sabou: a roadside attraction of only dubious spiritual significance, with an arbitrary admission fee and a nearby *buvette* selling refreshments. I knew Dafora was different, though, as soon as I smelled the blood.

We rented bicycles in the sprawling Bobo market and took the south road out of town. The road quickly slimmed into a dirt path skirting the edges of yam fields. Farmers, bent over crops, raised their heads at us as we rattled past. We sped along, making breezes out of the thick afternoon heat. We raced each other, as boys are obliged to do, until the road ended on the top of a cliff face. A steep footpath wound down to the ravine below, and we watched as four women, with pails of water balanced on their head and infants strapped to their backs, made their way up the path. "Dafora?" we asked, pointing into the ravine. They nodded. We waited for them to pass before locking our bicycles together and descending the path ourselves.

The trail led through the forest to a small clearing next to a deep pond. The area was cool and dark, shaded by thick trees and the walls of the cliff. The pond, however, was lit by a wash of sun pouring through a break in the canopy. It glowed green in the relative darkness. The scene might had been idyllic were it not for puddles of clotting blood and white feathers that covered the ground like gruesome snow drifts. Gore lent the air a sickening metallic stink and my sandals, blood-sticky, collected feathers as I walked. I felt queasy and wished I'd worn my boots. We peered into the pond but could see nothing save the thick, green murk.

A Burkinabé family arrived, carrying a live chicken by its legs. They walked to a small bloodstained altar built into the cliff wall. We watched from a distance, oddly nervous, as they began a solemn ritual of prayers, chanting and song. Then one man, a holy man of some sort, held the chicken to the altar, drew a large knife and slashed off its head. He carried the bleeding bird, still jerking, away from the altar to a spot on the ground. There, while another man built a small fire, the "priest" sliced open the chicken and scooped its warm innards into a calabash with his fingers. A new pool of blood formed and added another layer of stench to the air. A woman began plucking the feathers from the corpse as the priest brought the bowl of guts to the edge of the pond.

The priest whispered some prayers over the water, reached into the bowl and flung bits of entrails into the pond. Nothing happened. He prayed again and made another offering. This time, as soon as the guts slapped against the water, a giant catfish surfaced and gulped them down. I shuddered; its head was the size of a basketball. The priest tossed in another scoop of innards and this time three of the monstrous fish swam up to accept the sacrifice. The priest smiled, encouraged, and continued the feeding. When his bowl was empty he turned it upside down and shook it to let the last few drops of blood fall into the water. Then he looked up at us and grinned. The ritual was a success.

The priest returned to the rest of the family who roasted the chicken on the fire and ate it before leaving the clearing. In the meantime we watched another group of devotees arrive and repeat the ritual. This time, though, no fish surfaced. Bits of chicken entrails floated briefly on the surface before disappearing under the murk. The holy man looked dejected, and carried his empty bowl back to the others shaking his head.

Either the spirits were angry, or the sacred fish were full. After the trances in Glidgi, the dancing ghosts at Lake Aheme and the twins in Ouidah, I wasn't sure which to believe.

The end of December neared, Olivia and the Americans took their vacations in Togo, and I was left alone in Ouagadougou. As the holidays approached I was awash in homesickness, surprised that I, a reputed Scrooge back home, missed the Christmas chaos.

It was hard to find Christmas in Ouagadougou. There are few Christians in Burkina Faso; the Burkinabé are famous among West Africans for resisting Western religions. Even Islam, which has a devout following in the surrounding areas, managed to attract only about a quarter of the Burkinabé. The vast majority believed in ancient animist spirits. Still, since Ouagadougou is home to a large population of French expats, Christmas lights were sold in the marketplace and familiar decorations lined the café and grocery store windows where the wealthy *française* tended to shop. What did the locals think of the December fascination with a fat man in red and strange spiny trees?

Even with these holiday trappings—and the sudden appearance of thin-skinned oranges in the market—the setting didn't lend itself to Christmas feelings, especially for a boy from Calgary. Instead of snow, the *harmattan* wind blew sand and dust down from the Sahara making skies hazy and eyes itchy. In the hot afternoons I struggled to stay cool while back home my family huddled over cups of steaming chocolate and wore layered woollen sweaters. I missed the cold. I never thought I would.

One night at The Wassa Club, an Ouagadougou bar I frequented, a singer performing old jazz standards had to explain to the mainly Burkinabé crowd what the song "Autumn Leaves" was about. Few had ever heard of "autumn," much less "leaves of red and gold."

Feeling sentimental, I visited the Canadian Embassy in search of a Christmas party. The woman at the reception said there was going to be a dinner at the ambassador's home on Christmas Day and all Canadians in Burkina were invited. I considered attending but thought that my filthy backpacker garb and long tangled hair would be out of place at a soirée for diplomats and embassy staff. Further, the party was supposed to be a potluck and the only kitchen I could use was the one at my low-rent hostel. Cooking in that trash-heap would have necessitated flicking rat droppings off filthy cookware and competing with cockroaches for counter space. I decided to look elsewhere.

My map revealed a Benedictine monastery near Koubri, a small village a few kilometres south of the capital. Spending Christmas with African monks was an exciting opportunity, so on Christmas Eve I made my way south. I rattled the final seven kilometres to the monastery on the back of a moped belonging to an old villager. My chauffeur knew of *les frères* but had never heard of Christmas. A robed monk greeted me at the gate and listened to my sad story about my far away family and holiday loneliness. Smiling, he invited me in. He showed me to a simple room for pilgrims and handed me a schedule of prayers, services and meals. I had just enough time to wash before donning my best African clothes—the burgondy embroidered oufit I received in Denu—and head to the church for Christmas Mass.

The church was jammed with worshippers, and there were only about a dozen white faces among them. I never guessed Burkina Faso held so many Catholics. Excited to attend what promised to be an unforgettable ceremony I squeezed myself onto a bare piece of bench.

The ceremony was in Mossi, one of several local languages. I didn't understand a word, yet I found my body remembered the mechanics of the liturgy. I couldn't sing the Mossi songs or recite the prayers but my knees knew when to bend and my head, remembering, bowed itself. Language was incidental; the rite was as familiar here as in my old church back home. No matter how far removed I become from my childhood faith—both in time and geography—my bones recollect. Catholicism is a tattoo.

But only the structure of the mass was familiar; Christmas Mass in Koubri is a wholly African affair. Parishioners were dressed in bold and colourful African prints. Music was performed on indigenous drums, rattles and koras. Hymns were not mere translations into Mossi of the old familiar carols but were rich and entrancing African spirituals. I remember the music clearest of all, how it soared and wrapped itself around us all like smoke. The melodies and rhythms rose through the ground from the centre of the earth and flowed into my lungs, making them swell. My body wanted to sing the songs my head didn't know. Instead I rocked and swayed in my seat like a cradled child. A troupe of actors performed a nativity pantomime, complete with overacting innkeepers. When the holy couple lifted the infant Jesus over their heads the congregation threw their arms to the sky and cheered. I shook with unexpected bubbles of piety. Drummers' brows gleamed sweaty and their hands moved too fast to see. At the altar five women—with closed eyes and faces upturned as if into rain—danced to the *djembe* drums and *balafons*. Bats perched and soared in the rafters like surrogate angels.

The celebration lasted nearly two hours and left me tremulous. Afterwards, as men and women shook hands and kissed cheeks, boys lit firecrackers outside. I thought of my mother, thinking how much she would have enjoyed this Mass, and how happy she would have been that I was in a church on Christmas.

I was the only visitor at the monastery so the monks invited me to their private celebration. We gathered in the dining hall where small dishes of biscuits and roasted groundnuts were passed around, and tin kettles poured cups of tea and Nescafé. The normally serious and quiet monks talked and laughed loudly. Their white robes, usually hanging still and reverential, flowed around them as they slapped each other's backs and smiled *bonne fêtes*. Afterwards the monks returned to the church for the day's last devotion. The loud joys of the mass gave way to the tranquility of final prayers. Low chanting filled the space where hymns had soared an hour before, and instead of a dozen drums only a single kora played.

I fell asleep to thoughts of home and Mossi carols. It took the firecrackers following the morning mass to finally wake me.

I spent Christmas Day in the company of the monks. In celebration, French wine and jugs of indigenous beer accompanied both lunch and dinner. Still, we ate in silence, holiday or not. We gathered for another small *fête* in the afternoon, more biscuits and tea. A French monk with a long Claus beard asked me about my family, and the night's bats hung sleeping in the trees above.

The next morning, before walking to the main road to hitch a ride back to the capital, I went to the dining hall for my last monkish meal. Breakfast was cold leftovers. I smiled at this, remembering home.

When I returned to Ouagadougou, I found transport west to the Mali border. I stopped first in Bobo-Dioulasso for a final dinner at Restaurant Togolais, my favourite restaurant in Burkina Faso. I avoided meals at my hotel's restaurant where the specialty was horse meat. Three American travellers came in, and when they saw I was alone, they asked me to join them. When I sat and told them I was from Canada one of them asked, "Is your name Marcello?"

It turned out I was a minor legend. The Americans had come from Niger where they spent a few days in one of the Peace Corps hostels. The volunteers told stories of a long-haired Canadian who dug dinosaur bones in the desert and nearly died of malaria in the Maradi hostel. I hardly recognized the man they were describing.

Mali

I have been waiting in this taxi park for three uneventful hours. But now I'm watching a man who has a live crocodile slumped across his shoulders.. He walks to the centre of the lot, places the animal on the ground and waits. Both remain silent until a curious crowd gathers. The man dares anyone to give the reptile a coin. For a while, no one moves, each waiting for somebody else to take the crocodile man's dare. Finally somebody tosses in a coin. The crocodile snaps to life and charges into the crowd in the direction the coin came from. The crowd screams and scatters, delighted. The man bends to pick up the coin, lifts the croc back on his shoulders and walks away.

After spending twenty-five hours aboard two buses I finally made it to Mali. I arrived in Bamako and wondered why the overcrowded capital of one of the world's poorest countries smelled so good. Perhaps I had been in Africa too long, but the aromas of this city made me hungry.

It was difficult to find cheap accommodation in Bamako. The

French Catholic mission often housed travellers but the nun at the gate told me there would be no empty beds for several days. She directed me to a local woman, Fanta, who rented out rooms in her home. The house was under renovation—with business booming Fanta was adding a second floor to accommodate even more visitors—but she had a few beds available. She led me to a stuffy room filled with mosquitoes, pointed at a limp mattress on a broken frame and, without smiling, extracted my rent.

There was one other traveller staying in the room. When I entered he put down his book and we exchanged greetings. He was a Swede named Thomas and had been in Bamako for a few days.

"Are you a backpacker, too?" he asked. I looked at Thomas' luggage: a leather suitcase and an enormous duffel bag.

"I guess so," I nodded. Thomas returned to his book. He was reading Lee Iacocca's autobiography.

I arranged my things on the bed and changed into my sandals. I said to Thomas, "I'm heading out to find the post office but afterwards I want to check out the market and the National Museum. Do you want to join me?"

"No thanks. Actually I want to stay and finish my book."

"Are you a big fan of Chrysler?" I asked.

"Not really," he said, not looking up from the page. "Actually, I found the book under my bed."

On my way out I passed Fanta who was barking instructions at the builders on the roof. When she saw me she called me over.

"Is that boy going with you?"

"You mean Thomas?" She nodded. "No, he wants to stay in his room and read."

Fanta shook her head. "I do not like that boy. He is a very strange boy. He has been here five days and never leaves the room. He makes me nervous, that boy. He is very, very strange."

I tried to decipher the French labels on ancient drums and sculptures at the museum and wandered in the Bamako marketplace, amazed at the noise and smells of the crowds. I saw a man trying to sell a single jar of mayonnaise. He stood on a busy street corner, held the jar over his head and shouted, "Mayonnaise!

Mayonnaise!" at everyone who passed.

Bamako is friendly and hospitable, quite a relief from aggressive Ouagadougou where I always felt on the verge of a fight. I grabbed a seat on a *bâche*, a covered pickup truck, and headed towards the Canadian Embassy. The driver forgot to tell me when to get off, and we reached an outlying village by the time he realized I was still in the truck. I readied myself for anger but the driver apologized, returned my money and flagged down another truck to bring me to the embassy. After Burkina's hassles it was a joy to be treated with politeness again.

I became enamoured of the women in the city. The women in Bamako were dangerously pretty, and I spent much of the day trying to keep from staring. I remembered the desert women in Niger who were so intensely beautiful they took my breath and the thought of touching them made me afraid. I felt as if touching them would prove them unreal and ruin the fantasy. The Bamako women were beautiful in a different way. They were curved and sexy. Bright eyes and smooth skin. I wanted to touch them.

I picked up a stack of letters from the post office: Christmas cards, photos of Halloween and missed birthday parties. I also bought a strip of postage stamps commemorating Princess Diana's demise. She died less than three months before; Mali Poste was quick on the spoils of celebrity deaths.

When I returned to Chez Fanta several hours later Thomas was still on his bed. The book was almost finished.

"Did you visit the marketplace?" he asked. I told him I did and he sat up, suddenly interested. "Actually I was wondering what they are charging for bags of cement."

I waited for a punchline but none came; he just sat there staring at me with genuine interest. "I don't know, Thomas. I didn't ask."

"I see." He paused. "Do you know the prices for sheet metal?"

"No. I'm not in the market for building supplies. Why do you ask?"

"No reason. Actually I was just wondering." He returned to Iacocca.

Later, after he finished the book, we talked a bit about our time in Africa. Thomas had been travelling for a couple of months and made his way to Mali through Ghana and Côte d'Ivoire. I asked him how he managed on public cars and buses with such heavy bags.

"Actually, I only packed one hundred items into my luggage. Look, I listed them on a piece of paper."

He showed me his inventory list. It was neatly typed on white paper, double-spaced. It included a terry cloth bathrobe, five pairs of heavy blue jeans and four white shirts. I looked around the room. Three shirts hung crisp and pressed from clothes hangers around the room. The other, impossibly clean, was on Thomas.

"Actually, I don't like it when my clothes are wrinkled," he said. Looking distastefully at my patterned cotton trousers he added, "And those African-style pants are not for me." He examined his inventory list before carefully folding it and returning it to his suitcase. "I'm afraid in only six weeks I've already lost ten articles."

"I'm sorry, Thomas," I consoled.

When he was in Abidjan, Côte d'Ivoire's capital, Thomas stayed in a hotel in Treichville, one of the most dangerous neighbourhoods in West Africa. One night, at about two in the morning, Thomas decided to go for a walk—even soldiers don't walk in Treichville after dark. He had his camera around his neck, a wad of cash in his pocket and was robbed by a gang of thieves in about five minutes. Four of his ten missing items were lost in this encounter.

A crazy woman in Denu believed invisible enemies followed her around town. Another man jogged through the streets everyday wearing only his underwear. In Maradi, I met one of the town lunatics who decorated his home with epithets to former American president George Bush, Sr.. I met Thomas the Swede in Bamako.

I travelled from Bamako to Mopti, a lively town that is an important crossroads for travellers and merchants of all kinds. Here trucks from the larger cities of Bamako and Ségou, and from across the border in Burkina Faso, meet to exchange passengers and merchandise. Long gondola-like *pinasses* ply the Niger River carrying goods as far afield as Gao. The marketplaces offer *farako* tea from Niono, Timbuktu tobacco and huge slabs of salt from the mines at Araouane. Persistent guides and hustlers accost travellers en route to the famous market in Djenné or east to Dogon Country's dizzying cliffs. I stayed in a hotel-brothel where I met a drunk would-be guide staggering through the bar looking for clients. He said his name was John Travolta but I didn't believe him. On the hotel stairwell perfume-soaked prostitutes sat like potted plants. They grinned expectantly at me as I stepped past, whispering flatteries. In Mopti everything was for sale.

I spent a couple of days in Mopti before seeking transport to Bandiagara. I reached the Mopti motor park early in the morning, found a truck headed my way and bought my ticket, but the truck didn't move for eight hours. I passed the time watching a group of firewood merchants unload wood from an enormous truck, flinging logs from the top of the vehicle and letting them crash onto the ground. When we finally left the motor park we drove as far as the outskirts of Mopti—a journey of five minutes—before stopping for repairs. Half an hour later we were finally on our way to Bandiagara.

Along the way, we stopped to let a few passengers out in Sévaré. While they unloaded their belongings I saw three young boys sitting in the shade of a nearby mosque. With eyes closed tight in concentration, and with holy texts in hand, they recited the Quran. I listened as they recited Arabic poetry from memory, quick and rhythmic like a train, into the sounds of dusk.

Back on the road we travelled another hour or so until our truck suffered more troubles, this time with one of its wheels. Lacking a jack, our driver piloted the truck halfway into the ditch to elevate the offending wheel. He and his attendants quickly removed and repaired the wheel but, mysteriously, they could not reattach it. It was three hours before the crew of amateur mechanics managed to refasten the wheel to the truck. In the meantime the sun set, the stars emerged, and women gossiped. I could tell we were near onion fields by the smell of the air.

Once the problem was solved we returned to the truck and reached Bandiagara. The road from Mopti is only seventy-five kilometres. It took fourteen hours. I hardly noticed. I used to dread the three-hour journey to Accra from Denu. Now my patience felt bulletproof.

Bandiagara is on one end of the Bandiagara Escarpment, a series of dramatic cliffs that gently curve for 125 kilometres in southeast Mali. The escarpment is home to the famous Dogon people. Their picturesque villages and elaborate culture make Dogon Country—as it is known to everyone but the Dogon themselves—a popular destination and the biggest cog in Mali's almost cogless tourist industry. Dogon Country's popularity means the associated hustlers are almost as legendary as the region itself, and for this reason I had decided to give Dogon Country a pass. When I mentioned this intention to Olivia in Ouagadougou, however, she was bewildered.

"You cannot go to Mali and not visit Dogon Country," she said. "Would you go to Egypt and skip the Pyramids?"

I arranged my Dogon Country trip at my hotel in Bandiagara. Costs for my guide, accommodations and food for the six-day trek were expensive. I offered my watch as part of the transaction to reduce the price a little. Mom would have been upset if she knew I bartered away the watch she sent, but it had been months since I last needed to know the time.

In the morning, after tea and omelets, my guide Omar and I made our way from Bandiagara to the foot of the escarpment. Omar was quiet and friendly. With his ski jacket and Stars-and-Stripes baseball cap he looked as much a tourist as a guide. Only the ritual scars on his forehead suggested he was from Africa and not from the West. Where he found a ski jacket in Mali was a mystery to me; why he would wear one in such heat was another.

We wound our way from the top of the cliffs to the valley floor, passing through tiny villages with enormous names while Omar pointed out the Dogon architecture. Every wall was made of reddish mud, cracked by the sun and reptilian in texture. He showed me simple mud mosques, meeting places for men and thatch-topped granaries that sat on stilts to protect from thieving mice. We saw wandering goats and singing children. Village elders, looking a thousand years old, greeted me from the shade of a thick thatch canopy and asked for kola nuts. On the outer edge of Djiguibombo Omar showed me the rough structures where menstruating women must reside until they are "clean" again.

During the trek, Omar told me about the Tellum people who populated the escarpment before the Dogon arrived. The Tellum were pygmies and expert climbers who built their tiny homes and granaries high on the vertical cliffs in an attempt to dissuade invaders. Eventually, the Dogon unseated them by destroying their fruit trees and starving them down from their cliffside dwellings. The Tellum emigrated out of Mali and into central Africa. The famous Congo pygmies are their descendants, Omar said.

We paused in a small village at the bottom of the cliffs. After sharing a lunch of rice and sauce Omar led me to an empty room where I could rest. After napping for an hour I woke and found Omar in an adjoining room, alone, drinking out of a plastic jug. He looked up at me with reddened eyes and slurred, "Marcello! You are awake. Did you sleep fine?" Omar was drinking *konjo*—a local beer brewed from millet—and was quite drunk. I chatted with him as he emptied the rest of the jug.

While Omar slept off his buzz I walked out into the sandy plain that stretches from the foot of the escarpment to the horizon. Leaning against a baobab tree, I listened to village women pound millet and watch the cliffs change colour in the shifting, hazy daylight. At the edge of the village a four-year-old girl helped her younger brother struggle out of his T-shirt, his only clothes. Both naked, they bounded out of the village to play in cool *harmattan* wind.

We woke early the next morning, and by the afternoon Omar and I had already hiked for fifteen kilometres. We made our way slowly to the village of Yabatalu high atop the rocky plateau. The day's trek was strenuous as we strayed from the flat lowlands to ascend the escarpment itself, sometimes scrambling vertically up the cliff face. Even with my expensive hiking boots and a life of summers in the Rocky Mountains I felt unsure of my footing, but Omar, with nothing but cheap flip-flops on his feet, moved swiftly up the rock and made me envious of his dexterity. We climbed over boulders and through crevices almost too narrow for my pack, and our movement was soundless but for my heavy breathing and the constant slap of Omar's sandals against his heels. Emerging from canyons we faced walls of rock, or a misplaced field of orange sand dunes. We paused in Guimini and were greeted by village elders, serious women and children who repeated "*ça va*" in high-pitched voices that sounded like birds. After hours of climbs and descents I couldn't tell how high we had ascended from the sandy lowlands, or how close we were to the sky. The trail was difficult and unmarked, and I marvelled again at Omar who wound his way through the terrain as if by instinct, as if being Dogon means secret maps are written on his cells.

Eventually we turned a corner and faced a grand expanse of sky. The village of Dourou is perched on the top of the escarpment and from there my view would have stretched eastward to the end of the world if the vista hadn't been blurred into sepia by the dusty winds. We ate and rested, then descended the cliffs again to Nombori. There I washed my socks, which smelled like ammonia, before going to sleep.

In the morning we left Nombori and walked along the foot of the escarpment, climbing the lower reaches of the cliffs. In one village Omar showed me a cave where the Dogon bury their dead. Inside, ritual offerings shared the shade with human remains. A skull faced us from the shadows, and Omar got nervous when I took a photo. In another village I saw a simple church—a small mud building with a wooden cross over the door. Omar told me French missionaries built it. I asked him how many Dogon are Christian. "None," he said.

Later, Omar climbed into a nearby village to check if there was any food for us. I waited next to a freshwater stream. The shade and the cool water imparted a freshness to the air that I hadn't felt in weeks. Below me a Dogon man, clad only in shorts, soaked baobab cords in the stream. He was old and thin and his arms strained with the heavy wet bundles. After several days the baobab fibres would be soft and malleable. The man would weave them into ropes and sell them at the local markets. On the other bank three women with sleeping children strapped on their backs washed laundry. They sang to themselves until one of them noticed me watching. She made a joke and the others laughed. The rope man, balancing barefoot on slippery, wet stones, never looked up from his labour.

When we reached Yabatalu we shared a dinner of rice and sauce with one of Omar's uncles. Considering the amount of bone bits in the sauce it seemed Dogon butchers slaughtered their goats by running trucks over them. The next day, as we readied ourselves for our trek, Omar's uncle prepared himself for his own journey. He was walking south to Bandiagara. Travelling alone he carried only a small leather bag, a grass mat for sleeping and a large pear-shaped gourd filled with water. He would reach Bandiagara in about three days. When he saw my camera he insisted I photograph him. He faced my lens serious and unsmiling, wearing a white knit cap and a pair of sunglasses that seemed out of place on his face. All the while two dusty children finished last night's leftover rice, and one of Omar's teenage cousins carved a rattle from a baobab pod.

Each village along the escarpment devotes one day per week to *konjo*, the local millet beer that Omar so enjoys. On "*konjo* day" the village brewer prepares the *konjo* at dawn and it continues to ferment for the rest of the day. By late morning it is ready to drink, but it tastes best in the early afternoon and is spoiled by nightfall.

When we arrived in Tiréli, a little after noon, Omar whispered to me, "Do you want to drink *konjo*?" I followed him through Tiréli's narrow streets to the *konjo* house, the home of the village brewer. A large group of villagers were already gathered. They sat around the edge of the compound while the "*konjo* lady" hovered over a large clay vessel. The crowd, foggy-eyed and blissed, received me with curious yellow smiles. Tiréli is a popular stop for trekkers but few foreigners, it seemed, join the weekly *konjo* festivities. Two men waved at me to join them, shifting in their places to make room for me to sit.

One man drank from a calabash. He emptied it, wiped his lips and passed it to the *konjo* lady. She refilled the calabash and handed it to me. I looked inside. The brew was suspiciously cloudy and inhabited by specks of vegetation, a fair bit of sand and three blissfully drowning flies. I looked up at the boozy crowd; every glassy eye was staring. I smiled weakly and sipped.

The *konjo* was delicious. It was warm and flat, but smooth and pleasantly bitter. It also had a noticeable alcoholic bite. My eyes must have betrayed my pleasure because when I looked up from my beer, the villagers laughed and clapped. They urged me to finish quickly—*konjo* isn't for sipping, especially when there is only one calabash to go around. I tipped it back and poured the rest of the still fermenting liquid down my throat, flies and all.

I sat with the villagers until sunset emptying the calabash every time it came my way. The *konjo* tasted better and better on each pass; whether this phenomenon was due to its continuing fermentation or my dulling senses I am not sure. Around me women cackled drunkenly and old men told stories. Even the children were drunk. I watched a group of ten year olds stumble out of the *konjo* house and chase a goat around the village, laughing madly. Some called out "*ça ba, ça ba,*" their drunken corruption of the French greeting. The party continued until darkness, when everyone weaved their way home.

I went to bed a bit hazy, dreading what would be my first millet hangover.

With heads mildly aching we left Tiréli on our way to Banani, but Omar was nervous. He told me the day's trek would bring us past the village of Yaye where a local ritual was underway. Each year the Yaye village chief removes one of Yaye's sacred fish from a special pool in the village. Special prayers are performed, then the chief carries the fish out of Yaye to the nearby road. He does this every day for twenty-eight consecutive days. The chief waits at the junction for someone to pass then he offers him the fish.

"You will die if he gives you the fish," explained Omar.

"I don't understand," I said. "Is the fish poisoned?"

"No. You do not eat the fish. You will die if you are only offered the fish."

"What if the person does not take the fish?"

"It does not matter. If you are only offered the fish, your death will come. Every year people die like this."

Omar, petrified, insisted we detour around Yaye instead of taking the main road. "It will be long, but we will be safe." I didn't object.

A kilometre north of Tiréli we met another guide, a friend of Omar, leading a pair of Europeans. Omar warned him about the dangers at Yaye, but the man shook his head.

"No, no, no. There is no worry. The chief waits until afternoon before he brings down the fish. It is still early. As long as you pass before noon there is no problem."

Omar was still nervous but we accepted the man's advice and continued along the main route. As we neared Yaye Omar became quiet and quickened his pace. I had trouble keeping up. When we passed the Yaye junction I smiled at Omar but he looked straight ahead of him, sweating a little. After a couple of kilometres he stopped, rested his hands on his thighs and exhaled deeply. He looked over his shoulder.

"We passed Yaye," he breathed and put a hand on my back. "Marcello, I was very afraid. My heart is beating too fast."

Safe from deadly fish we continued to Banani at a more relaxed speed. This was the strangest danger I'd ever been in.

The cliffs became more dramatic as we travelled north, and the ancient Tellum buildings were so high I sometimes had to squint to see them. At such a height they looked like bird nests—homes for eagles, not men.

I tried to imagine the Tellum climbing these cliffs. Maybe they used ropes made from baobab fibres. Maybe they used no ropes at all, crawling vertical the way insects do, their hands and bare feet feeling the rock for secure holds, their fingers and toes armoured with calluses. What did the women do, I wondered. Did they climb, too, with their long dresses hiked up and infants strapped to their backs? Did they ever fall? I imagined the slow motion plummet, the panicked screams, then the sickening silence.

In the evening the sun's fading made me happy. In Dogon Country I looked forward to the ends of days almost as much as their beginnings. Stretching out on the flat rooftops brought relief to weary legs and fatigue inspired serenity. My Mopti blanket cut the chill of the cool, dry air. My jacket, rolled up and tucked under my head, was my pillow. Each night I lay on my back under a sky of stars just out of my reach. Meanwhile, village sounds made strange lullabies. One night a man chanted prayers into the darkness. On my last night in the escarpment I heard a distant stereo playing a Beatles cassette. *Rubber Soul*, I think.

When I returned to Mopti, I booked passage on a small boat headed north along the Niger River. I would spend three days on the water. I was going to Timbuktu.

On the morning of my departure, as I packed my bag for my voyage north, I heard a woman's voice speaking English below my window. She was an American woman, blonde and pretty, chatting with a group of children who surrounded her and begged for candy and coins. A few minutes later I heard her settle into the room next to mine. I waved at her through her open door on my way downstairs. She smiled, and for a moment I wanted to stay in Mopti. I nearly abandoned my plans just to test the possibilities in her smile. Looking back it seems so foolish. Months without that kind of companionship weakened me, I guess.

My boat was loaded with sacks of rice and sugar and would return from Timbuktu with salt from the northern mines. There were two other foreigners aboard, Hans and Mariam, a pair of forty-something Dutch hippies. We represented more exotic, but less valuable, cargo.

Hans and Mariam were a joy. Hans sold used clothing and marijuana in Amsterdam. He had a son, Sasa, named after a character from a Malian folk tale. Mariam was a big chatty woman, a nurse, who spent her life travelling. She crossed the Sahara Desert three times back when the old routes through Algeria were safe, and told wild stories of her travels through the Middle East and North Africa.

Mariam insisted on sharing the details of her intimate hygiene. She kept Hans and I updated, for example, on the colour and quantity of her urine: "Yesterday I only passed two and a half cups. Do you think I'm dehydrated?" I love the Dutch.

There were about a dozen local men on the boat, but they scarcely talked to us, only calling over occasionally to ask Hans for cigarettes. They spent most of their time drinking tea and listening to scratchy cassettes of Malian storytellers, or *griots*, who tell funny stories accompanied by some sort of whining African violin. The men played the same cassettes over and over again, laughed at the same parts and never grew bored. All the while our captain steered the craft through the water while his "first mate" checked the water depth with a long pole.

I spent my days sprawled out on sacks of cargo reading books or writing in my journal, or sitting shirtless on the roof of the boat, risking burns for a tan. Hans taught me to smoke the carved pipe I bought in Dogon Country, but the Malian tobacco was too harsh for my beginner lungs. Still, the sting of local weed made me feel more a part of the place. We slipped past riverside villages and waved back at the women and children who crowded the banks to watch us pass. Reflections of birds skimmed across the river. Fishermen tossed nets into the water from tiny canoes with torn sails.

The boat stopped once each afternoon to allow everyone aboard to climb ashore and find a place to shit. Pissing off the boat was commonplace—I tried to forget that the river was also our source of drinking and cooking water. Defecating over the side, however, was taboo. On these stops, everyone pulled their trousers high and splashed overboard. The riverbed ooze tugged at our feet and one morning the thick mud sucked one of my sandals off. I spent three minutes standing awkwardly on one leg and probing the muck with my toes before I found it again. Once on dry land we each searched for a dune or bush that might afford some privacy. Passengers last off the boat had to walk further afield to find a private spot, passing the other squatters and pretending not to notice them.

On one of these daily defecations, I learned never to squat behind a thorn bush.

Nights were cold and somewhat uncomfortable. My thin blanket provided little protection against the cool river breezes, and the bit of plank I slept on was angled slightly towards the side of the boat. The fear of a nocturnal roll into the river kept me from sleeping soundly. Further, many of the men aboard were observing the Ramadan fast, so once the sun set they spend much of the night eating, smoking and playing music.

But the days' beauty made up for nightly discomforts. The boat passed through Lac Débo on our second morning on the water. Each riverbank receded from view, and at the horizon the still water and cloudless sky met at some invisible junction. The *harmattan* haze surrounded everything in an indistinct whiteness and softened all edges. For three hours we floated like this, without the certainty of perspective. I couldn't tell the water from the sky. Only the ripples at the side of the boat betrayed we were moving at all. We hovered in white silence, as if in a cloud. Mariam napped. Hans finished smoking some marijuana out of my pipe and silently said the rosary. In the front of the boat, most of the men slept while our captain kept the *pinasse* slipping silently northward.

For months I enjoyed travelling on backfiring bush taxis, and learned to love the rattle and clamour of people and chickens— Africa's cacophany was a stimulant. But this boat offered the opposite pleasure: tranquility. The world became soundless, but for the click of Hans' beads. I was so still I could feel my heart beat deep inside. People told me there was nothing to see in Timbuktu, that there was little to the town but its mythical name. Regardless, the peaceful days on the river made the journey worthwhile. Besides, where else did I have to be?

There were only two hotels in Timbuktu, and both were expensive.

Luckily, one of the restaurants in town called La Poulet d'Or allowed travellers to stay in a small shed next to the kitchen. I slept on a grass mat laid over the sand and used my blanket as a pillow. It was the most comfortable I'd been in weeks.

Strange posters decorated the walls at La Poulet d'Or. I'd seen these posters all over West Africa. They were made in Nigeria and depicted, among other things, soccer superstars, Nigerian cabinet ministers, heroes of Islam, military aircraft and grisly scenes from African massacres. Others were tributes to Western celebrities like Michael Jackson and Princess Diana. Most of the posters, however, were odd pin-ups featuring young Asian models. The photos were hardly titillating: models smiled demurely and rarely exposed more than an inch of flesh. The ridiculous captions, often in misspelled English, were great fun. One of the Poulet d'Or posters, entitled "Sugar Girl" and depicting a Japanese girl in a red kimono, read

"B" for Beauty!
Beauty is your fine physical image. It is the baby of
your mind, your confidense and your positive
posture. It is the pure perfection of your
appearanse. Beauty is cleanliness...and cleanliness is
next to Godliness. Beauty lyes in the eyes of the
beholder. Just be beautiful!

"B for Beauty." It reminded me of Ouidah and Monique's earrings.

Timbuktu was like no place I'd been, and I pity those who said there was nothing to this place; how sad to be so devoid of imagination. In the morning I followed the smell of fresh bread to the clay ovens that stood on every street. I was only there a couple of days before I found a favourite baker. Each morning she put a few hot loaves aside for me and wrapped them in paper so I didn't burn my hands. Timbuktu is known for its whole wheat bread. When it was hot and smothered with jam it was easy to forgive the grains of sand that invariably found their way into the dough and crunched in my teeth.

I walked in the streets each afternoon, passing bored donkeys and brushing my fingers along the ornate wooden doors that make the buildings seem more Arabic than African. Faded signs pointed to tourist attractions like the crumbling homes of European explorers, or ancient mud mosques. From one building I heard children chanting verses from the Quran, the suras streaming out of an open window. I walked through the voices as I would a sunbeam. Quranic verse is beautiful and rich and there were times I wanted to be Muslim just to have that poetry in my mouth. Later, the Quranic school let out and children flowed through the heavy doors into the sandy courtyard. Squinting and laughing, they hardly noticed me watching.

A holy man gave me a tour of the Sankoré Mosque. A small boy accompanied him, holding a small bag of sand. The boy opened the bag periodically to allow the man to spit into it.

"It is Ramadan," he explained when I questioned him. "During the day, Muslims are forbidden to pass anything down their throats. No food. No water." The man spit to keep from swallowing his saliva and breaking the holy fast.

I stole sunsets from the top of dunes on the outskirts of the city. I climbed barefoot to feel the fine sand ooze between my toes. Around the edges of town were small camps composed of large domed tents made of woven straw mats. The grey straw matched the colour of the sand and the tents looked as if they were growing out of the ground—desert bubbles. The same tents were found in town, occupying the empty space that resulted from an abandoned house that dissolved into sand.

Nights were truly magical. The garish light of day emphasized the city's crumbling, its slow but steady decay into sand, but in the shadows, Timbuktu remained grand and mysterious. I spent evenings getting blissfully lost and imagined the secrets guarded by dark corridors. The quiet darkness intensified nocturnal noises. The sounds of children playing and men praying. Old radios. Donkeys. Sometimes light charged out from an open door. Inside, families dined under high ceilings by the light of kerosene lamps, or single bulbs hanging from wires. During the day I could hardly hear Timbuktu whisper, the light was so loud; by night I felt it breathe on my neck.

Some nights I walked to Hotel Bouctou to drink beer in the stuffy bar, or to watch the tourists lose their patience with aggressive guides and souvenir sellers. Countless peddlers patrolled the tables on the popular terrace in search of customers to overcharge. The salesmen and guides rarely approached me. Compared to the well-heeled "adventurers" who come to Timbuktu by plane and can afford the pricey rooms at Bouctou I was not an attractive consumer. My shabby sandals and long tangled hair meant I was ignored for a change.

However, my hair did attract some attention. A man in a shining white *boubou* and matching turban sat down next to me at the bar. He touched my hair and made a face.

"This hair is no good," he said, fingering tangles. "It is long, like a woman. I will fix it for you, no problem. My name is Boubacar, The Famous Barber of the Sahara. The only barber in Timbuktu who knows white man's hair."

He opened a case filled with brushes and scissors and removed a thick envelope. Inside were photos of freshly shorn Europeans, with Bouboucar smiling, scissor-armed, at their side. There was also a stack of postcards. Clients from around the world wrote praise and thanks for Boubacar's skills.

"You see," he said, selecting one card in particular. "This one is from Canada. He is from Toronto."

I politely declined Boubacar's services. My "Africa hair" was one of my favourite souvenirs. For the first time in my life I was hairy and unkempt. I felt free and wild.

One of the Tuareg camel guides joined me in the bar one evening. He was weary of canvassing for clients on the terrace, so he came inside and collapsed in the seat next to mine. I expected him to begin a sales pitch so I sharpened all my French rebukes, but he didn't try to sell me anything. Instead he adjusted the metre-long sword on his belt, and whispered *"bon soir"* through the turban folded over his nose and mouth.

I returned the greeting and asked to see his sword. His eyes smiled. He untied the weapon from his waist and unsheathed it for me, pointing out three long grooves that ran the length of the blade.

"These represent the three major routes that cross the desert," he said. "The Tuareg love the desert."

Speaking through cloth he told me about his father and uncles and their long treks through the Sahara. He told me about camel races and how to bake bread in the sand. He told me that even when business is bad, like that night, spending time in the dunes gave him great pleasure. I told him I loved the desert, too, but as soon as I spoke, I felt foolish. His adoration was generations deep. Mine was just a crush.

I had originally planned to "market-hop" my way back to Mopti from Timbuktu. A string of small villages near Timbuktu held their weekly markets on consecutive days, and I hoped to take advantage of the resulting traffic and hitch my way south. It was to be an exciting journey, I thought, but it was thwarted by a Muslim holiday. The month of Ramadan ended, and during the celebrations markets were postponed. Every truck was still. I had to wait for the festivities to end to find a ride.

It was interesting to be in Timbuktu for the Feast of Ramadan. Islam follows the lunar calendar and a particular phase of the moon determines the end of the month-long fast. For days before the feast men pressed their ears against radios for official reports by Islamic astronomers. At night every head tilted towards the sky. On the morning of *la fête* the city was deserted as everyone crowded into the mosques for prayers. Afterwards I watched them stream into the streets. Women wore colourful dresses and headcloths, their faces shining with heavy makeup. Men in shimmery robes or flashy shirts shook hands with those sweating inside Western-style suits and ties. The festive colours were brighter against the sepia landscape, and in the heat perfumes and colognes seemed more pungent. Young girls in pretty dresses and boys in smart shirts wandered the dust demanding coins, *cadeaux* for the feast. My favourites were a pair of young brothers wearing identical grey suits but no shirts.

I heard music and celebration from behind closed doors and hoped that someone would invite me to join their festivities. No one did. Some things, I suppose, were not for me.

The faces were beautiful, but I'll never be able to show them to anyone. People did not want to be photographed. I laugh when I think that my albums suggest Timbuktu is a city of abandoned streets and crumbling mosques, populated only by donkeys. One must endure the heat and dust and shabby hotels to marvel at these faces. My memories, then, are my reward for coming here.

After the feast I found transport back to the capital aboard a smoke-spewing dragon of a truck. The vehicle carried about twenty passengers, most of whom were laid out in the bed of the truck along with their baggage. Since the driver forced me to pay an exorbitant price for the ride, I demanded to sit in the cab, in *la premier place*. This was a mistake. There were three passengers crammed into the cab—in addition to the driver—and I was pressed against a passenger door that would not close properly. Only a bit of frayed rope kept the door from swinging open and dumping me on the ground. At a police checkpoint a stern soldier examined the door and warned me, "You will surely fall." I could do nothing but shrug my shoulders and hope he was wrong.

On the way out of Timbuktu, a crazy woman stood in the middle of the road stopping our truck. She was bare-breasted and demanded a toll before she let us pass. The driver shouted playful curses at her until she gave up her enterprise and moved off the street. Everyone had a good laugh.

In spite of the uncomfortable ride, the view from the cab was incredible. I wouldn't have seen anything from the high-walled bed of the truck. On the first day we travelled in the desert along *piste* roads that were little more than faint tracks in the dust. Four times our tires sank and stuck in the soft sand, and I had to help the other men dig the truck out. We passed groves of Y-shaped trees, shallow lakes and grazing camels. When we joined the main road a herd of long-horned cattle blocked our route. We waited as they lumbered past, goaded by two boys who couldn't have been more than eleven years old. Sand dunes shone in the distance.

We stopped to rest in nearly every town we passed and slept in rough shelters next to motor parks. The villages were beautiful and rustic, with charming names like Tonka and Dioura, places I would not have chosen to visit but was thrilled to see. The locals were friendly and curious—they don't receive many foreigners in these tiny places. We stopped in Niafounke, the hometown of musician Ali Farka Toure. If I had known we'd be there for five inexplicable hours I would have tried to find him.

In Niono, a town famous for its *farako* tea, I endured another long and unexplained delay. I spent much of the day in the marketplace buying tea to bring home and chatting with the music sellers. I bought a stack of Malian music cassettes, but my cassette player was ruined. Timbuktu sand jammed the mechanisms. While I shopped five old men pored over my tattered map of Mali, fascinated.

After three days on the truck, I finally reached Bamako. I visited the Mauritanian embassy to obtain a tourist visa. The official examined my passport, looked up at me, then at my passport again. He told me to wait and called for his supervisor. The supervisor checked my passport and frowned. He held it out to me, pointing to the photo and said, "Is this you?"

I laughed when I saw it. The photograph showed a man with short-cropped hair, a clean shaven face and thick neck. I had changed so much. My hair had grown long and unruly, and a tangled beard hid much of my face. My skin was darker, my neck thinner and it looked like I'd lost twenty pounds.

"Yes that's me," I said. "At least it used to be."

"When was this photo taken?" he asked.

"Last March. Eleven months ago."

"That is quite a transformation."

Mauritania

A bush taxi crammed with passengers arrived this afternoon. Among them was a German man in his late forties. He stepped out of the car and stretched his cramped legs. When he saw me he came over and introduced himself.

"Where did you just come from?" I asked.

"I've come down from Fdérik. In the north. Where the ore mines are."

"That's the middle of nowhere. What were you doing there?"

"Just travelling," he said. "How long have you been in Africa?"

I told him that I've been travelling for ten months, and that I am flying back to Canada in a couple of days.

"Is this your first trip?"

I nodded.

"That's a good trip." He smiled. "I've been travelling all my life and I want to tell you something. You will not understand anything about your trip until you return home, and sit, and think. And it will take a long time. Right now you don't know anything."

He shook my hand and sat back in the taxi with the other passengers.

The driver revved the engine and he disappeared down the road to Atâr. I'm not sure I really saw him.

I found transport across the stretch of desert that separates Mali from Mauritania in Nara, a border town where girls in shells, beads and braids returned my smiles with suspicion. I joined about fifteen other passengers in the back of a pickup truck. There were two other foreigners aboard, a pair of Syrian tourists in button-down shirts and dark slacks. One looked just like my uncle Mike.

Our driver filled the back of the truck with baggage. The passengers sat on top and gripped the taut ropes that held the cargo in place. Everyone gathered close to the centre of the truck bed, trying to avoid being near the edge in case of a sudden bump which would cause people to tumble overboard. I was one of the last aboard the truck, unfortunately, with my seat dangerously close to the brink.

Behind me sat an elderly man with a young granddaughter on his lap. During the trip he kept shifting to make himself more comfortable, each time nudging me towards the edge. I warned him that if he kept shoving I would fall out of the truck. He just grinned and said, "*Pardon moi, Monsieur.*"

The ride was magical. Our driver followed faint tracks on the ground—there was no road. We saw lonely mud homes with families that waved at us as we rattled past. I watched the sunset drip red all over the sand, and the full moon so bright our driver never clicked on the headlights. The *harmattan* wind had eased, and the sky was clear and thick with stars. In order to see them more clearly I tried to clean the filth from my eyeglasses, but the air was so dry that my breath could not fog the lenses.

During the ride I wondered, really wondered for the first time, why I was doing this. Why was I travelling? I'd been in Africa for nine months, filling journals and building castles of memories, but I'd never asked myself why. I'm still not sure. Sometimes I wondered if it was all about finding stories to tell, about painting myself as a grand adventurer, making myself more interesting—never revealing the secret that anyone can do these things, that I was not as special and intrepid as I wanted to seem. Maybe I was creating reasons for people to love me—love me for my stories and my photos, for my African clothes and jewellery, for my malarial blood and the Saharan sand caught by the corners of my pack. Love me for the things I saw and the things I did.

These were back-of-truck musings. Tumbling over the uneven ground, it felt like we were at sea. Such movement always lulled me into philosophy and coaxed introspection.

That is, until I plunged overboard.

The fidgeting man pushed me again. I lost my grip on the ropes, pitched forward and fell headfirst off the moving truck. I landed on my face in the soft sand and lay still for a moment to determine if I was injured. I let my body feel itself for pain and broken bones. Luckily, I'd only cut a finger. I stood, shook the sand from my hair and beard, and walked, enraged, back to the truck which stopped a few metres away. Uncle Mike and the others were scolding the man, but he held up his hands innocently. I charged up to him and shook my fist in his face, shouting English obscenities that he didn't understand. Nine months in francophone Africa and I still couldn't lose my temper in French. Yelling at an old man with a young frightened girl made me feel foolish, however, and my temper quickly fizzled. The other passengers put their hands on my shoulders to calm me down, and shifted to make a spot nearer to the centre of the truck where I'd be safe. When I climbed aboard a man smiled, shrugged and brushed the sand from the back of my shirt. The old man never apologized.

We arrived in Timbedgha at two in the morning. This was not where I was supposed to be, and it seemed I'd inadvertently broken a handful of immigration laws. I thought the journey would end in Néma where a customs post could validate my visa and legalize my presence in Mauritania. There was no customs post in Timbedgha. Further, it was forbidden to import Mauritanian currency into the country. My transaction with a money-changer in Nara, as it turned out, was criminal. Fortunately, the lone man at the Timbedgha police post was sleeping next to a collection of empty beer bottles when I arrived—interesting, considering alcohol is outlawed in Mauritania. He was either too tired, too drunk or too hungover to care about my several infractions and quickly stamped my currency declaration form before returning to his mat. I feared, though, that there would be trouble when it came time for me to leave Mauritania. I decided to save a few American bills in case I needed to bribe my way home.

I spent that night on a mat next to the highway. I was not alone. About a dozen men were there, laid out for the night in hopes of finding transport in the morning. At one of the roadside shops I bought some fresh bread, but a goat stole it while I slept, then stepped on me and fled down the highway.

The Sahara Desert is a slow ocean. Nothing, and nobody, moves quickly there. Dune waves, carved by desert winds, can take years to shift. Camel caravans plod for weeks to bring salt slabs from deep desert mines. Mauritanian women amble along the streets like floats in a parade, slowed by their colossal girth and draped with bright fabric. My months on the desert edge purged me of my Western haste and taught me to slow down.

In the desert drinking tea is a ceremony of slowness, a rite nobody dares rush. I'd taken tea with wealthy Moorish business-men, with silver merchants and in front of tents with black-tur-baned nomads. Their languages changed from place to place. Even their flesh was darker here and lighter there. But everywhere the ritual of tea was the same: three tiny cups, never more or less, each sweeter than the one before.

After I reclined with my host, whoever he may have been, on floormats and cushions, a small boy would be sent to fetch coals. There were always *petits* nearby to perform such tasks, as if they sat just outside shop doors or tent flaps to perform the errands of dig-nified old men. While he rushed to the marketplace, a tiny pot would receive water and a handful of Chinese "gunpowder" tea. My host would place the teapot on a wire basket of glowing coals, and we might chat while we waited for the water to boil.

When the water began to bubble, my host would lift the pot from the coals, protecting his fingers from the heat with a shred of cardboard. He'd pour the tea into a glass and shake the wet tea leaves out of the pot. His fingers might disappear inside to search for clinging, fugitive leaves. He'd put aside the tea leaves, pour the tea back into the pot and add a bit of sugar. The pot would be returned to the coals and we'd wait for the tea to boil again.

My host would raise the pot high above a glass and pour the tea in a long elegant stream. Then, he'd return the tea to the pot and pour again. He'd do this over and over, his movements as precise and graceful as a dancer's, until the tea was cool enough to drink. It is a miracle he'd never spill. The tea would splash from such a height that it granted each cup a crown of bubbles which we'd noisily slurp away. Our cups were scarcely larger than shot glasses and often my host would empty his quickly. I was usually afraid of burning my unseasoned lips and took longer to finish. The first cup was always bitter and strong, and my host would tell me the proverb *The first is bitter like Death.*

My host would begin the ceremony again, adding fresh water to the pot and reusing the wet tea leaves. Once it boiled he'd remove the tea leaves and add several spoonfuls of sugar. Again he'd splash the tea into our cups from a raised teapot, and again we'd slurp off the bubbles. The recycled leaves and extra sugar mellowed the brew. *The second is long like Life.*

The same tea leaves would be used again for the third pot. While it boiled my host would pluck mint leaves from their stems. A small pile of green usually formed between us by the time the water was ready. He'd added the mint leaves to the pot and increase the amount of sugar. By the time the tea boiled again the mint had turned the tea to gold. It was thick and syrupy yet somehow refreshing in the heat of the afternoon. *The third is sweet like True Love.*

When I think of my time in the desert I cannot help but think of tea. The fresh smell of mint cutting the dry air. The flavours of bitter and sweet slipping across my tongue. The ember's dull red glow. My senses will not forget these slow, cross-legged hours. The tea's splash and the click of teapot lids were the musical score of these desert days. I felt warm as ordinary things turned sacred and wondered why my days in Canada were so devoid of ritual.

There are other "tea proverbs." My favourite was told to me by the friendly Moor in Kiffa who gave me a place to stay: the first glass represents the frailty of friendship and the second the bonds of family.

But the sweetest is always love.

I arrived in Choûm, fumbling out of a crammed Peugeot with a thick layer of dust inside my lungs. I'd come from Chinguetti where I'd sat on amber dunes and looked over my shoulder as light winds melted away my footprints, renewing contours. Chinguetti is nearly a thousand years old. I was nearly twenty-five.

I had been travelling in West Africa for over eleven months. By the time I'd reached Choûm I was out of money and out of time. Noadibhou would be my last town, Choûm my last village, and the train that linked them, the last passage across the sands I'd fallen in love with.

I followed the other taxi passengers to the nearest "garage" where we waited for the train. In Mauritania rough structures called "garages" were found near motor parks and highways where those in transit, mostly men, might have to stop for the night. Garages were shelters for people, not vehicles; the Mauritanian equivalent of a highway motel. A typical garage is a three-walled shed made with rough wood and sheets of corrugated steel. Here commuters can sleep and chat on thin mats, and take water from communal barrels or hairy water-skins made from unlucky goats. There was always a general store, or *boutique*, nearby where supplies such as sandy bread, biscuits and tins of sardines were for sale. I bought water, powdered milk and sugar to make *zrig*, a sort of simple liquid meal that was oddly delicious. A friendly Moor "with some English" taught me about *zrig* at a garage in Néma. Still, I preferred the rice and sauce sold by the quiet women who sweated endlessly over pots and fires.

Getting around Mauritania on public transport was a slow occupation, and I'd spent many nights in garages waiting for a morning truck or midnight taxi. I hardly minded these pauses. The kindly Moors offered me tea and handshakes, and often invited me to share their dinners. They didn't see many foreigners in these places and I was treated like a guest.

The garage in Choûm was lit by a single kerosene bulb, which created more shadows than light, and was attended by an enormous Moor woman making tea for the travellers. After my pupils opened to the darkness I could see the other men in the room. Some were sleeping. Others were gossiping over tiny cups of tea. I left my boots in the doorway and found a spot in the darkness to lay down.

My arrival caused a stir among the others in the garage. At first I thought they were surprised to see a foreigner so far from the capital. I was used to this and paid little mind to their muttering and glances. But soon I realized their reaction to me was more menacing than curious. Many of the men grumbled angrily and pointed in my direction. I had no idea why.

A man approached. He frowned down at me, pointed to my feet and said something in Hassiniya. I couldn't understand. I removed my shoes before I entered the room, according to custom, so I couldn't imagine what sort of foot faux pas I had committed. I shrugged my shoulders. He shook his head and pointed at my feet again. Surely he didn't expect me, an obvious stranger, to understand every intricacy of Moor etiquette. And typically, my social gaffes were a source of amusement for the locals; they never caused this sort of commotion. Annoyed, I shrugged my shoulders again.

But when he waved his hand in front of his nose I understood, and I felt my face redden—he was telling me that my feet stunk. I hadn't broken some obscure Moorish taboo; I simply smelled bad. I could hardly blame those men. I hadn't bathed in well over a week and had been wearing the same pair of sweat-stiff socks for almost as long. And since I had been travelling alone I had no one to tell me of my growing aroma.

Embarrassed, I smiled like a fool and mumbled a French apology. The man made me stand and follow him to the doorway of the garage, then signalled me to wait. While I stood there I tried to avoid the eyes of the other men in the room. I looked down, but seeing my feet made me even more ashamed, so I stared at a wall instead. After a moment the man returned with a small plastic basin of water and a sliver of soap. I thanked him and reached for it. He shook his head and knelt in front of me. He made me lift each foot so he could tug off the offending socks, then proceeded to wash my feet. I protested, offering to do it myself but he ignored me. Perhaps he had little faith that I knew how—my stench was cause for doubt. So I stood there, feeling guilty and foolish. When he finished he dried my feet with a bit of rag, tucked my socks into my boots and pointed to my spot in the garage, giving me permission to return. I whispered "*merci*" and went to sleep.

At three o'clock in the morning one of the younger men in the garage woke me. "*Monsieur*, the train is here."

"I thought the train comes in the afternoon."

"It is true. The passenger train comes tomorrow. But you can take this train, if you like. There is no car for passengers. You must sit on top of the iron ore."

"Is that safe?"

"It is very cold and there is some risk, but the ride is free."

I sat up and reached for my bag. This was a rare opportunity to save a little money. But when I felt the chilly air I laid back down. I was in no real rush to get to Nouâdhibou, and certainly in no hurry to put my socks on again, so I opted for sleep and the relative comfort of the afternoon train.

I woke in the morning to a commotion outside the garage. The young man who had woken me brought me news.

"The afternoon train will be delayed. Last night the train fell off the rails, and they have to remove the cars and repair the tracks. It will take some time."

"Last night's train derailed?"

He nodded.

"The same train that I was going to take at three o'clock? The train where people sat on top of the iron ore?"

"Yes."

"Was anyone hurt? Was anyone on top of the train when it derailed?"

He didn't know.

"What if I had taken the train last night?"

He laughed nervously at this question. "I do not know. It would have been bad." Then he walked away.

The derailment meant the train was delayed. Nobody knew how long we'd be stranded in Choûm. One man said it would take a week for the rails to be repaired. Another predicted five days. One optimistic man was certain the train would arrive before sundown. The ambiguity made me ill-tempered.

Further, my insides started to rebel against some toxin or another—perhaps I should have avoided the goat-head stew—and I spent much of my time making urgent dashes out of the village. There were no toilets in Choûm. As far as I could tell the wasteland that surrounded the village acted as its vast latrine and, it appeared, its dumping ground for dead livestock. The ground was littered with the decomposing bodies of goats and camels. When nature bid, everyone simply wandered out into the field of corpses and thorns to find a convenient squatting place. For the locals privacy was not an issue; long robes doubled as curtains for such activity. My trousers did not offer this luxury, so a private shit required a long march. I trampled over animal carcasses in varying degrees of rot. Some still had sticky eyes buzzing with flies. Others were reduced to bones by insects and bleached white by sun. Camel hides lay in heaps like dirty laundry. The nightmarish landscape matched my intestinal suffering. I blurted diarrhea over random skulls and splattered my sandals. I anchored bits of pink shitty toilet paper to the ground with stones. Delirious flies rioted around my feet.

I did this constantly for two days, and stared up at the tracks for the delayed train to rescue me and bring me to Noadibhou.

I don't know what I expected from my last African days. I don't know what sort of grand farewell I hoped for. Maybe I thought, foolishly, that the last few hours could sum up the months before, like the perfect phrase that ends a poem. I don't know what I wanted, but I knew it wasn't diarrhea and derailed trains. I knew it wasn't skulls and flies. I didn't want these months of wonderment to end in a coda of misery.

The wait was numbing. I had nothing to read but my worn guidebook. There wasn't much left of it. I scribbled in my journal and watched the others, not bothered by the delay, share tea and listen to scratchy radios. A group of men played *boules* in the sand with silver balls. Lacking any other amusement I made imaginary wagers on their games and ate bags of groundnuts.

Finally, someone told me the train was coming. Everybody in Choûm suddenly knew this, though I couldn't tell how. Squinting northward I couldn't see a train approach, no telltale plume of pollution or crying whistle. No official announcement was made. Just a rumour that quickly passed through the crowd, stirring sleepers and breaking up conversations. I grabbed my bag and followed the mob out to the tracks.

There was no train station in Choûm. Not even a platform. Not even a sign. The passengers simply gathered beside the tracks at a seemingly arbitrary spot of sand. There, a uniformed man collected money and handed out tiny paper tickets. I tucked mine into my pocket.

A few minutes later the train appeared on the northern horizon, clunking lazily towards us. When it came within five hundred metres of the crowd everyone began sprinting towards it. Sitting comfortably on my pack, I wasn't ready for this race; I thought the train would be coming to us. The majority of the passengers were elderly men and women weighed down with bags and tanks of propane, so I was able to catch up. Everyone raced for a specific car near the end of the train and nobody waited for the train to stop before grabbing onto a ladder and pulling themselves aboard. I guessed, correctly, that seating was limited. When I reached the car one of the younger passengers who was already aboard beckoned me to toss him my bag. Afterwards, he reached his hand out to help me up.

The passenger car was, essentially, a long empty box. Two long wooden benches that ran along either length of the car represented its only seating, and there were no windows save for two portholes on either side, each about the size of a paperback novel. I managed to secure a spot on one of the wooden benches. I was lucky because these filled quickly and the majority of the passengers—and certainly all of the women—were destined to sit on the bare floor. Once the car filled we began our slow clunk coastward. Nobody collected our tickets.

After about an hour a man stood to watch the sun out of the west porthole. The other men in the car stared up at him, quiet, waiting for his signal. When he turned and nodded it meant it was time for prayer. All of the men tried to stand at once, but the car was too crammed for synchronous devotions. They quickly agreed that half of the men pray first while the others waited for them to finish. I watched as men who scarcely had room to sit found space for the standing, kneeling and bowing movements that animate Muslim prayers. I watched them search for a spot of bare floor to touch with their foreheads, all the while whispering Allah's praises, their eyes closed. Then I watched again as the second group, getting impatient, took their turn.

Bowing. Kneeling. Standing. Hands to legs. Fingertips to temples. Forehead to floor. Arabic whispers floated in the air like angels. My body felt calm for the first time in days.

After prayers, about a dozen of the travellers lit small gas burners to prepare tea. The air in the train quickly thickened with the aroma of mint and tobacco smoke, which ascended in thick ribbons from the tiny ornate pipes that all men in the country seemed to smoke. Tiny cups were passed around the car, to both friends and strangers. Excited, I burned my lips on the first one. With the sun gone the only light in the car was provided by the jagged circles of blue flames from gas burners and the glowing pipe tips. The murmer of Hassiniya talk fell gently between the rattle and tap of the teapot lids.

A young woman in light blue robes giggled at some whispered

joke. When I looked at her she looked away, shyly tucking back the strands of black hair that fled her head scarf and anchoring the cloth around her ears to prevent such immodesty. I watched her for a little while, wondering if she would look back at me again. She never did.

Eventually it was time to sleep. The burners and pipes were extinguished and somehow everyone found room to recline. Each passenger made sure his neighbour had enough space to be comfortable. Such a spatial miracle could never occur at home, where physical closeness is a strict and senseless taboo. A man near me touched my shoulder and pointed to a tiny piece of floor where I could lay my head, and I became a part of this marvellous flesh jigsaw puzzle. We lay so close we shared each other's breath.

Stepping off the train the next morning I carried away the images of the journey—the shy girl, the tobacco smoke, the warm breath of strangers. On my plane home, as Africa sped away below me, I felt that night etched on my bones, the vibrations of the tracks beneath us thumping through our bodies like a second, shared heartbeat, carrying us to morning destinations.

I wish to thank all those who supported and encouraged me during the writing of this book, especially The British Columbia Festival of the Arts, The Canada Council, The Alberta Foundation for the Arts, my editor extraordinaire Jan Barbieri, and my friends and family.

Special thanks to Canadian Crossroads International for the opportunity, Gabrielle Cran for her belief, Ron Reive for his inspiration, The Planet for their coffee, Leanne Clare for her unsympathetic editing, the butterfly for the lessons, Jenn Chic for the map, Donna Dennis and the good folks of Quadra Island for their hospitality, Paul Sereno for his dinosaurs, the Niger Peace Corps for their emergency meds and, especially, Moonira Rampuri for her love.

I would like to extend my gratitude to the gracious and welcoming people of West Africa, particularly the staff and students of Three Town Senior Secondary School in Denu, Ghana.

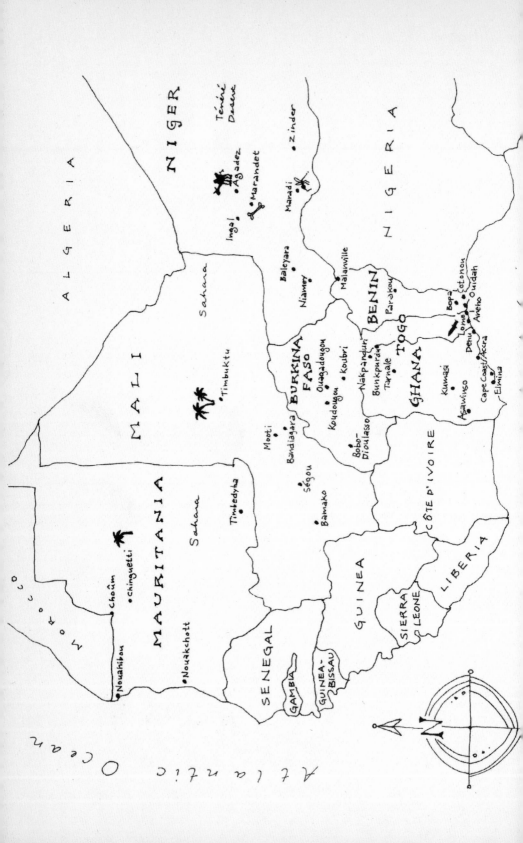